꼭 알아야 하는 영문법

8품사·문장성분·5형식

함동욱 저

개정판

SLA영어 북스토어

꼭 알아야 하는 영문법
8품사·문장성분·5형식
개정판

개정판 1쇄 발행 · 2025년 6월 16일
초판   1쇄 발행 · 2024년 8월 26일

지은이 · 함동욱
발행인 · 함동욱
기획/편집 · SLA영어북스토어 기획팀
디자인 · SLA영어북스토어 디자인팀

발행처 · SLA영어북스토어
출판사 등록일 · 2022년 7월 28일
주소 · 서울특별시 양천구 목동중앙남로 7-1 조오빌딩 2층
대표 전화 · 02)6012-5599

정가 12,900원

- 본 책은 저작권법에 따라 보호받는 저작물이므로
  무단전재나 무단복제 및 전송은 저작권법에 따라 금합니다.

ISBN 979-11-7158-732-2(53740)

Photo Credits
All photos © Shutterstock, Inc.

Copyright © 2025 SLA영어북스토어

Table of Contents

꼭 알아야 할 영문법
8품사·문장성분·5형식

8품사 – 내용 이해하기	4
8품사 – 실전문제	11
문장성분과 5형식 – 내용 이해하기	29
문장성분과 5형식 – 실전문제	49

workbook

8품사	80
문장성분과 5형식	95

정답 및 해설집

8품사	106
문장성분과 5형식	111

workbook

8품사	122
문장성분과 5형식	127

꼭 알아야 하는 영문법

8품사

8품사

영어의 기본적인 단위는 단어이며, 이 단어는 의미에 따라 8가지로 나누어지는데, 이를 8품사라고 한다.

8품사의 종류

01 명사: 사람, 동물, 사물, 장소, 눈에 보이지 않은 무형의 이름을 가리키는 말이다.

예) • 사람의 이름: Steven, Dr. Smith, teacher, student
     • 동물의 이름: cat, dog, zebra
     • 사물의 이름: book, chair, pencil
     • 장소의 이름: Chicago, Italy, park, school
     • 무형의 이름: air, water, happiness

Charles Puth is an American singer. 찰리 푸스는 미국 가수이다.
  사람의 이름

I like your **car**. 나는 네 차가 마음에 들어.
         사물의 이름

Jack lives in **Chicago**. 잭은 시카고에 산다.
        장소의 이름

Happiness is more important than money. 행복은 돈보다 더 중요하다.
 무형의 이름

02 대명사: 명사를 대신하여 쓰이는 말이다.

대명사는 크게 인칭대명사와 지시대명사로 나뉜다.

A. 인칭대명사: 주격, 목적격, 소유 대명사

인칭	주격	목적격	소유 대명사
1인칭 단수	I (나는, 내가)	me (나를, 나에게)	mine (나의 것)
1인칭 복수	we (우리는, 우리가)	us (우리를, 우리에게)	ours (우리의 것)
2인칭 단수	you (너는, 너가)	you (너를, 너에게)	yours (너의 것)
2인칭 복수	you (너희는, 너희가)	you (너희들을, 너희에게)	yours (너희 것)
3인칭 단수	he (그는, 그가)	him (그를, 그에게)	his (그의 것)
3인칭 단수	she (그녀는, 그녀가)	her (그녀를, 그녀에게)	hers (그녀의 것)
3인칭 단수	it (그것은, 그것이)	it (그것을)	없음
3인칭 복수	they (그들은, 그들이, 그것들은, 그것들이)	them (그들을, 그들에게)	theirs (그들의 것)

내용 이해하기

Nick is my classmate. **He** studies very hard. 닉은 나의 반 친구야. **그**는 매우 열심히 공부해.
He는 Nick를 대신하는 대명사이다.

I know Olivia and Nicole. **They** are good friends. 나는 올리비아와 니콜을 안다. **그들**은 좋은 친구들이다.
They는 Olivia와 Nicole을 대신하는 대명사이다.

B. 지시대명사: 주격과 목적격의 형태가 같음

	단수	복수
가까운 것을 가리킬 때	this (이것/이 사람)	these (이것들/이 사람들)
멀리 있는 것을 가리킬 때	that (저것/저 사람)	those (저것들/저 사람들)

This is my mobile phone and **that** is your mobile phone on the shelf.
이것은 내 휴대폰이고 선반 위에 있는 **저것**은 너의 휴대폰이다.

These are my blue jeans. **이것(들)**은 제 청바지입니다.

Those are my books. **저것(들)**은 내 책(들)이다.

03 동사: 사람이나 사물, 동물의 동작이나 상태를 나타내는 말이다.

예) • walk(걷다), go(가다) 등은 사람의 동작을 나타나는 동사
 • be(~이다), feel(느끼다) 등은 사람의 상태를 나타내는 동사

She **walks** to school every day. 그녀는 매일 학교에 **걸어 간다**.
walks는 '걷다' 라는 동작을 나타내는 동사이다.

I **feel** sick. 나는 아프다. (아픔을 **느끼다**)
feel은 '느끼다'라는 상태를 나타내는 동사이다.

04 형용사: 명사의 성질, 모양, 수량, 색깔 따위를 나타내는 낱말로서 명사를 꾸며 준다.
형용사는 받침이 주로 '~ㄴ' 으로 끝난다.

예) beautiful(아름다운), handsome(잘생긴), kind(친절한), new(새로운), nice(좋은), red(빨간)

She is a **beautiful** girl. 그녀는 **아름다운** 소녀이다.
beautiful(아름다운)은 '소녀'라는 명사를 꾸며주는 형용사이다.

She is an **ugly** girl. 그녀는 **못생긴** 소녀이다.
ugly(못생긴)은 '소녀'라는 명사를 꾸며주는 형용사이다.

내용 이해하기

● **형용사의 위치**

A. 형용사 + 명사		
B. 주어	형용사를 필요로 하는 동사	형용사.
	be 동사 (am, is, are, was, were)	
	감각 동사 (feel, look, smell, sound, taste)	
	상태변화 동사 (become, get, grow, turn 등)	

A. 명사를 꾸며주는 형용사 (형용사+명사)

My **elder** brother is looking for a job. 나의 **형**은 직업을 구하고 있다.
I live in a **small** city. 나는 **작은** 도시에 산다.

B. 주어를 설명해 주는 형용사 (주어+be 동사+형용사)

Greg is **kind**. 그레그는 **친절**해.
The little boy is **asleep**. 그 어린 소년은 **잠들**어 있다.

> **주의** a-로 시작하는 일부 형용사는 명사 앞에 쓰이지 못하고 주어를 설명하는 역할로 쓰인다.
> 예) afraid(두려워하는, 무서운), alike(비슷한), alive(살아있는), alone(혼자 있는), asleep(잠이든), awake(깨어 있는) 등
> ~~Jenny is an afraid girl.~~
> ~~It's an asleep boy.~~

C. 감각 동사나 상태변화 동사와 함께 사용하는 형용사 (주어+감각/상태변화 동사+형용사)

The bread tastes **great**. 그 빵은 **맛있**다. (감각 동사+형용사)
I became **nervous** before the interview. 나는 면접을 앞두고 **긴장이** 되었다. (상태변화 동사+형용사)

● **-ly로 끝나는 형용사**

대부분의 부사는 -ly로 끝나지만 명사에 -ly를 붙이면 형용사가 되는 경우

명사	형용사
cost 비용	costly 비용이 많이 드는
friend 친구	friendly 다정한
love 사랑	lovely 사랑스러운
time 시간	timely 시기적절한

*friendly-~~friendily~~ lovely-~~lovelily~~ 같은 부사 형태는 없다.

I like his **friendly** smile. 저는 그의 **다정한** 미소를 좋아해요.
She is a **lovely** girl. 그녀는 **사랑스러운** 소녀입니다.
Your advice was **timely**. 너의 조언은 **시기적절**했어.

내용 이해하기

05 부사: 동사, 형용사, 다른 부사, 문장 전체를 수식하는 말이다. 부사는 주로 '~하게', '~히'라고 해석한다.

예) happily(행복하게), nicely(좋게), really(정말), slowly(천천히), today(오늘), very(매우)

● 부사의 역할

A. 동사 수식

I walked **slowly**. 나는 **천천히** 걸었다.

부사 slowly(천천히)가 동사인 walked(걸었다)를 꾸며주고 있다.

B. 형용사 수식

He is **really** smart. 그는 **정말** 똑똑하다.

부사 really(정말)가 형용사 smart(똑똑한)를 꾸며주고 있다.

C. 다른 부사 수식

She speaks **very** quickly. 그녀는 **매우** 빠르게 말을 한다.

부사 very(매우)가 다른 부사 quickly(빠르게)를 꾸며주고 있다.

D. 문장 전체 수식

Unfortunately, he didn't pass the exam. **불행하게도**, 그는 시험에 통과하지 못했다.

부사 Unfortunately(불행하게도)가 문장 전체를 꾸며주고 있다.

● 부사의 종류

A. 방법 부사: 행동이 어떻게 이루어지는지 나타내고 주로 형용사에 -ly를 붙인다.

예) quickly(빠르게), slowly(느리게), softly(부드럽게) 등

They walk **quickly**. 그들은 **빠르게** 걷는다.

B. 시간 부사: 행동이 언제 일어나는지 나타낸다.

예) now(지금), today(오늘), tomorrow(내일), yesterday(어제) 등

Please, stop writing **now**. **지금** 쓰는 걸 멈추세요.

C. 장소 부사: 행동이 어디에서 일어나는지 나타낸다.

예) everywhere(어디에나), here(여기), inside(안에), there(저기) 등

Come **here** for a minute. 잠시 **여기로** 오세요.

내용 이해하기

D. 정도 부사: 동작이나 형용사의 정도를 나타낸다.

예) much, so, very(매우, 무척) 등

Thank you very **much**. 매우 감사합니다.

E. 빈도 부사: 행동이 얼마나 자주 일어나는지 나타낸다.

예) always(항상), usually(주로), often(자주), never(결코 ~가 아닌)

I will **always** love you. 나는 너를 항상 사랑할게.

● 형용사와 부사의 형태가 같은 단어

early	(형) 이른 (부) 일찍, 이르게	Italy is lovely in **early** June. 이탈리아는 6월 초에 정말 아름다워. The train arrived **early**. 기차가 일찍 도착했습니다.
fast	(형) 빠른 (부) 빨리, 빠르게	Tim caught the **fast** train to Rome. 팀은 로마행 고속 열차를 탔다. Slow down. You're driving **fast**. 속도를 줄여. 너는 빨리 운전하고 있어.
hard	(형) 단단한, 어려운 (부) 열심히, 단단하게, 세게	The table is **hard**. 그 테이블은 단단하다. It's **hard** to believe that the concert is already sold out. 콘서트가 이미 매진되었다는 사실이 믿기 어렵다. Frank works **hard**. 프랭크는 열심히 일한다. Hit it **hard**. 세게 쳐.
last	(형) 마지막인 (부) 마지막으로	It was my **last** opportunity. 이건 나의 마지막 기회였다. When did you **last** hear from Sam? 너는 마지막으로 샘에게 연락을 받은 게 언제였니?
late	(형) 늦은 (부) 늦게	Liam is **late** today. 리암은 오늘 늦네. He arrived **late** this morning. 그는 오늘 아침에 늦게 도착했다.
long	(형) 오래된, 긴 (부) 오래, 길게	The bridge is very **long**. 그 다리는 매우 길다. How **long** will it take to get there? 거기에 도착하는 데 얼마나 오래 걸리나요?
pretty	(형) 예쁜 (부) 꽤, 상당히	Jenny is **pretty**. 제니는 예쁘다. It's **pretty** cold today. 오늘 꽤 춥다.
well	(형) 건강한 (부) 잘	I am **well**. 나는 건강해. The car runs **well**. 그 차는 잘 달린다.

● -ly를 붙이면 의미가 달라지는 형용사와 부사

bad	(형) 나쁜, 좋지 않은	She got a **bad** grade on her test. 그녀는 시험에서 나쁜 성적을 받았다.
badly	(부) 나쁘게, 심하게, 몹시	She was **badly** hurt in the accident. 그녀는 사고로 심하게 다쳤다.
hard	(형) 어려운, 단단한	This exam will be **hard**. 이번 시험은 어려울 거야.
hard	(부) 열심히, 단단하게, 세게	He worked **hard** all day. 그는 하루 종일 열심히 일했다.
hardly	(부) 거의 ~하지 않는	I can **hardly** hear you. 난 너의 얘기가 거의 들리지 않아.
high	(형) 높은	The prices at that store are **high**. 그 가게는 물건 값은 높다(비싸다).
high	(부) 높이	The kite flew **high** in the sky. 연은 하늘 높이 날아갔다.
highly	(부) 매우, 대단히, 높이 평가하여	The movie is **highly** recommended. 그 영화는 매우 추천된다.
late	(형) 늦은	I was **late** for work. 나는 직장에 늦었다.
late	(부) 늦게	Ellen has to work **late** tonight. 앨런은 오늘밤에 늦게까지 일을 해야 한다.
lately	(부) 최근에	I haven't seen him **lately**. 나는 최근에 그를 본 적이 없다.
quick	(형) 빠른	I had to make a **quick** decision. 나는 빠른 결정을 내려야 했다.
quickly	(부) 빠르게	She finished the assignment **quickly**. 그녀는 과제를 빠르게 마쳤다.

내용 이해하기

06 **전치사:** 명사나 대명사 앞에 놓여 다른 말과 관계를 나타낸다. 전치사란 우리말에 조사라고 할 수 있다.

예) at(~에), for(~를 위하여), in(~안에), of(~의), on(~위에)

I live **in** Seoul. 나는 서울에 산다.

영어에서 in은 전치사이지만, in은 우리말에 '~에' 해당하고 '조사'라 불린다.
우리말에서 조사는 명사 뒤에 위치하지만 영어에서 전치사는 명사 전에 위치한다.

Goodbye! See you **on** Sunday. 잘 가! 일요일에 보자.

on은 '~에'로 해석되며 Sunday라는 명사 앞에 놓인 전치사이다.

07 **접속사:** 두 개 이상의 같은 종류의 말(단어, 구, 절)을 연결해 주는 역할을 한다.

예) and(그리고, 및), but(그러나), when(~때), while(~하는 동안)

A. 단어와 단어를 연결하는 접속사

I like apples, bananas **and** tomatoes. 나는 사과, 바나나와 토마토를 좋아한다.

위의 문장은 bananas와 tomatoes의 두 단어를 연결해 주기 위해 접속사 and가 사용되었다.

I play tennis, baseball **and** soccer. (O) 나는 테니스, 야구와 축구를 한다.
I play tennis ~~and~~ baseball and soccer. (X)

and는 마지막으로 나열된 단어 전에 사용해야 한다.

B. 구와 구를 연결하는 접속사

▶ 구: 두 단어 이상이 함께 쓰여 새로운 의미를 만들지만, 그 안에 '주어+동사'가 있으면 안된다.

He washes the dishes, **but** doesn't clean the floor. 그는 설거지는 하지만 바닥 청소는 하지 않는다.

위의 문장은 'washes the dishes'와 'doesn't clean the floor'의 두 동사구를 연결해 주기 위해 접속사 but이 사용되었다.

C. 절과 절을 연결하는 접속사

▶ 절: '주어+동사' 구조를 갖고 있으며, 문장 안에서 하나의 성분처럼 쓰인다. 혼자서는 독립적인 의미를 갖지 못하고, 다른 문장의 일부로 사용된다. 접속사를 사용하여 절과 절을 연결할 수 있다.

<u>I listen to music</u> **when** <u>I am down</u>. 나는 우울할 때 음악을 듣는다.
    주절   종속절

'I listen to music'은 주어와 동사가 있는 문장으로, 단독으로도 사용할 수 있다. 하지만 위 문장에서는 종속절 'when I am down'과 함께 쓰이며 주절의 역할을 한다. 위 문장은 접속사 when이 두 절을 연결하여 하나의 완전한 문장을 만든 것이다. 'I am down' 역시 주어와 동사가 있어 문장이 될 수 있으나, 접속사 when이 붙으면 종속절이 되어 주절과 함께 사용되어야 한다.

내용 이해하기

08 **감탄사: 감동, 놀람, 응답, 부름 등의 말로서 감탄사는 독립적으로 문장 앞에 쓸 수 있다.**

예) oh(어, 오), oops(아이고), wow(와)

Oh, look! There is a man on the roof. 어, 봐봐! 지붕 위에 어떤 남자가 있어.

Wow! That's a great car. 와! 정말 멋진 차다.

> ▶ 다의어: 하나의 낱말이 여러 가지 뜻을 나타낼 경우, 그 낱말을 다의어라고 한다.
> 한 단어가 두 개 이상의 품사를 가질 수도 있으므로, 문장 속에서 그 의미를 정확히 파악해야 한다. 의미를 이해하기 어려울 때에는 사전을 활용하는 것이 좋다.
>
> **watch**
> - 명사: I like your **watch**. 나는 네 시계가 마음에 들어.
> - 동사: I **watch** TV. 나는 텔레비전을 본다.
>
> 첫 번째 문장에서 'watch'는 '시계' 라는 뜻으로 명사 역할을 하고 있는 반면, 두 번째 문장에서의 'watch'는 '~를 보다' 라는 뜻으로 동사의 역할을 한다.
>
> **fast**
> - 부사: He ran **fast** to catch the bus. 그는 버스를 잡기 위해 빨리 달렸다.
> - 형용사: She is a **fast** runner. 그녀는 빠른 달리기 선수이다.
> - 동사: Muslims **fast** during Ramadan. 이슬람교도들은 라마단 기간 동안 금식한다.
> - 명사: I had a one-day **fast** for charity. 나는 자선을 위한 하루의 단식을 했다.
>
> 위 예문들처럼, 하나의 단어라도 문장에서 어떤 역할을 하느냐에 따라 품사가 달라질 수 있다. 또한, 어떤 단어의 품사를 잘못 파악하는 이유 중 하나는 그 단어의 정확한 뜻을 제대로 알지 못해서일 수 있다. 예를 들어, I am happy. 라는 문장에서 happy의 품사는 무엇일까? 많은 학생들이 'happy'를 '행복하다'라고 해석하면서 동사로 착각할 수 있다. 하지만 happy는 '행복한'이라는 뜻의 형용사이다.

실전문제

01 다음 단어들은 어떤 품사의 예시인지를 쓰시오.

A) really, slowly, very _____ B) I, you, they, hers, he _____

C) wow, well, oops _____ D) and, or, but _____

E) by, in, of _____

02 다음 밑줄 친 단어에 품사를 써 넣으시오.

A) She is a <u>beautiful</u> girl. _____ B) I live <u>in</u> Seoul. _____

C) I like your <u>car</u>. _____ D) <u>They</u> are friends. _____

03 다음 밑줄 친 단어에 품사를 써 넣으시오.

A) <u>Wow</u>! That's a great car. _____ B) I <u>feel</u> sick. _____

C) He is <u>really</u> smart. _____ D) I like apples, bananas <u>and</u> tomatoes. _____

04 다음 밑줄 친 단어의 품사는 무엇인가?

<u>**He**</u> will visit his grandparents.

① 명사 ② 대명사 ③ 형용사 ④ 부사 ⑤ 동사

05 다음 밑줄 친 단어의 품사는 무엇인가?

<u>**Hey**</u>! Put that down!

① 명사 ② 대명사 ③ 감탄사 ④ 접속사 ⑤ 동사

06 다음 밑줄 친 단어의 품사는 무엇인가?

<u>**Liam**</u> brought his notebook to class.

① 명사 ② 대명사 ③ 형용사 ④ 부사 ⑤ 동사

07 다음 밑줄 친 단어의 품사는 무엇인가?

She wore a <u>**new**</u> dress.

① 전치사 ② 접속사 ③ 형용사 ④ 부사 ⑤ 명사

08 다음 밑줄 친 단어의 품사는 무엇인가?

My father **or** I will pick you up from the airport.

① 전치사　② 접속사　③ 형용사　④ 부사　⑤ 명사

09 다음 밑줄 친 단어의 품사는 무엇인가?

Please help **us**.

① 명사　② 대명사　③ 형용사　④ 부사　⑤ 동사

10 다음 밑줄 친 단어의 품사는 무엇인가?

I **understand** your problem.

① 명사　② 대명사　③ 형용사　④ 부사　⑤ 동사

11 다음 밑줄 친 단어의 품사는 무엇인가?

We arrived **early**.

① 명사　② 대명사　③ 형용사　④ 부사　⑤ 동사

12 다음 밑줄 친 단어의 품사는 무엇인가?

You are **early** today.

① 명사　② 대명사　③ 형용사　④ 부사　⑤ 동사

13 다음 밑줄 친 단어의 품사는 무엇인가?

I saw him **last** night.

① 명사　② 대명사　③ 형용사　④ 부사　⑤ 동사

실전문제

정답 p. 106

[14-21] 〈보기〉 단어의 알맞은 품사를 써 넣으시오. **(총 23단어)**

〈보기〉 dog, on, bad, car, slowly, have, for, she, really, new, woman, this, big, and, eat, of, quickly, boy, it, wow, bed, oh, but

14 명사   dog

15 대명사   _____

16 동사   _____

17 형용사   _____

18 부사   _____

19 전치사   _____

20 접속사   _____

21 감탄사   _____

22 다음 빈칸에 알맞은 품사를 써 넣으시오.

I play baseball and volleyball.

① I _____   ② play _____   ③ baseball _____
④ and _____   ⑤ volleyball _____

23 다음 빈칸에 알맞은 품사를 써 넣으시오.

Keven and I love movies.

① Keven _____   ② and _____   ③ I _____
④ love _____   ⑤ movies _____

24 다음 빈칸에 알맞은 품사를 써 넣으시오.

Love is blind.

① Love _____   ② is _____   ③ blind _____

[25-29] 다음 밑줄 친 부분에 알맞은 품사를 써 넣으시오.

〈보기〉 **She** is **angry**.
　　　　대명사　　　　형용사

25 <u>He</u> is <u>very</u> <u>cold</u>.

26 <u>They</u> are <u>nice</u>.

27 <u>We</u> <u>like</u> <u>apples</u>.

28 <u>Wow</u>! Your <u>girlfriend</u> is <u>really</u> <u>beautiful</u>.

29 <u>I</u> <u>live</u> <u>in</u> <u>Tokyo,</u> <u>but</u> <u>he</u> <u>lives</u> <u>in</u> <u>Sydney</u>.

30 다음 밑줄 친 단어의 품사를 빈칸에 써 넣으시오.

　① Min-hee bought a new <u>watch</u> yesterday. _____

　② My brother <u>watches</u> TV every morning. _____

　③ I like this <u>shop</u>. _____

　④ I <u>shop</u> at K-mart. _____

31 다음 밑줄 친 단어의 품사를 빈칸에 써 넣으시오.

　① Snails are <u>slow</u>. _____

　② Jack, <u>slow</u> down. _____

　③ <u>Color</u> the picture. _____

　④ I like bright <u>colors</u>. _____

32 다음 밑줄 친 단어의 품사를 빈칸에 써 넣으시오.

　① He wore a gold <u>ring</u> on his right hand. _____

　② I <u>rang</u> the doorbell but no one came. _____

　③ Where do you <u>work</u>? _____

　④ There isn't a lot of <u>work</u> for me. _____

33 다음 밑줄 친 단어의 품사를 빈칸에 써 넣으시오.

① Water the plants regularly. _____

② I want to drink water. _____

③ Each lesson lasts an hour. _____

④ Mike saw her last weekend. _____

34 다음 밑줄 친 부분에 품사가 다른 하나는?

① I need to check the time. Where's my watch?

② I bought a new watch for my brother's birthday.

③ Let's watch a movie tonight.

④ I lost my watch while swimming in the ocean.

⑤ Can you lend me your watch? I forgot mine at home.

35 다음 밑줄 친 부분에 품사가 다른 하나는?

① She ran fast to catch the bus.

② He drives too fast on the highway.

③ She finished her work fast.

④ She is a fast runner and always wins the races.

⑤ They ate their meal fast because they were late for the movie.

36 다음 밑줄 친 부분에 품사가 다른 하나는?

① We watched a fantastic play at the theater last night.

② She plays the piano in her free time.

③ My kids often play hide-and-seek.

④ Will Miranda and Cathy play a board game after dinner?

⑤ The band will play their new song at the concert.

*hide-and-seek: 숨바꼭질

37 다음 밑줄 친 부분에 품사가 다른 하나는?

① She woke up early to catch the first train.

② The early bird gets the worm.

③ Olivia is early today.

④ It is early morning.

⑤ Italy is beautiful in early June.

실전문제

38 밑줄 친 부분을 알맞은 대명사로 바꿔 쓰시오.

> 대명사 (I   you   he   she   it   they   we)
>
> 〈보기〉 **Jack** is a student. = **He**

A) Kate is tired. = _____   B) Tom is a good boy. = _____

C) Denny and Tony are good friends. = _____   D) The doll is very cute. = _____

E) Judy and I are classmates. = _____

39 다음 주어진 단어를 대명사(주격)로 고쳐 쓰시오.

A) books = _____   B) Emma = _____

C) the room = _____   D) dad = _____

E) cars and ships = _____

40 다음 주어진 단어를 대명사(주격)로 고쳐 쓰시오.

A) Sam and Sue = _____   B) mom = _____

C) your aunts = _____   D) the school = _____

E) Min-ho and I = _____

41 다음 주어진 단어를 대명사(주격)로 고쳐 쓰시오.

A) your parents = _____   B) the sun = _____

C) my sisters = _____   D) his car = _____

E) you and my friend = _____

42 다음 주어진 단어를 대명사(주격)로 고쳐 쓰시오.

A) my dog = _____   B) you and your brothers = _____

C) Jack and I = _____   D) he and she = _____

E) my uncle = _____

43 다음 문장에서 명사에 모두 밑줄 치시오.

A) Jason likes the movie about France.   B) The musicians play great songs.

C) Boys and girls have the same chances.   D) A lot of people speak English.

44 다음 문장에서 대명사에 모두 밑줄 치시오.

A) You and John are the most important players.
B) Mr. Smith gave us the chocolate.
C) They sent it as a birthday gift.
D) Jack and I like eating them.

45 다음 문장에서 동사에 모두 밑줄 치시오.

A) They go to West Point and watch the parade.
B) Just do it.
C) It is a nice place. Many people go there on vacation.
D) She cried loudly, and both of us heard her.

46 다음 문장에서 형용사에 모두 밑줄 치시오.

A) You look great today.
B) My brother lives in a new house.
C) It is a large round table.
D) There are many beautiful yellow flowers in the garden.

47 다음 문장에서 부사에 모두 밑줄 치시오.

A) Watch very closely.
B) My team played badly.
C) Go slowly. Look carefully. Walk there.
D) Ah! The sun is so warm.

48 다음 문장에서 접속사에 모두 밑줄 치시오.

A) Lucy and Ed left the door open.
B) He is going to school, but I am going to work.
C) He studied hard, so he passed the exam.
D) You can have ham, cheese, or tuna.

49 다음 문장에서 전치사에 모두 밑줄 치시오.

A) The knife is on the table.
B) I will see you in the morning.
C) Columbus made his first trip from Europe to America.
D) When they were in China, they spent a few days in Beijing.

50 다음 문장에서 감탄사에 모두 밑줄 치시오.

A) Oops, I made a mistake again.
B) Hurray! We won the match.
C) Wow! Look at that!
D) Oh no, I forgot to turn off the stove!

51 다음 중 형용사를 모두 빈칸에 쓰시오.

China   late   brave   student   noisy   smart   young   easy

_____

52 다음 중 부사를 모두 빈칸에 쓰시오.

there   hardly   heavy   carefully   angrily   good   tired   different

_____

53 다음 중 전치사를 모두 빈칸에 쓰시오.

but   or   in   for   about   of   and   under

_____

54 다음 중 품사가 다른 하나는?

George, man, people, sick, paper, spoon, eraser

55 다음 중 품사가 다른 하나는?

really, lucky, easy, busy, real, final, happy

56 다음 중 품사가 다른 하나는?

at, on, in, for, about, and, from, under

57 다음 중 품사가 다른 하나는?

speak, go, learn, make, wash, strong, have

58 다음 중 품사가 다른 하나는?

sit, true, listen, do, know, forget, arrive

59 다음 중 품사가 다른 하나는?

very, really, slowly, certain, truly, quickly, easily

정답 p. 108 **실전문제**

60 다음 중 품사가 같은 단어끼리 짝지어진 것이 아닌 것을 고르시오.

① Jack – Seoul ② run – happy ③ really – gently
④ thin – great ⑤ true – healthy

61 다음 중 품사가 같은 단어끼리 짝지어진 것이 아닌 것을 고르시오.

① great – smart ② movies – Italy ③ finish – late
④ America – school ⑤ and – but

62 다음 중 품사가 같은 단어끼리 짝지어진 것이 아닌 것을 고르시오.

① easily – slowly ② of – with ③ oh – wow
④ handsome – beauty ⑤ kind – helpful

63 다음 중 품사가 같은 단어끼리 짝지어진 것이 아닌 것을 고르시오.

① strong – cute ② walk – visit ③ Jason – he
④ is – go ⑤ quickly – happily

64 다음 중 품사가 같은 단어끼리 짝지어진 것이 아닌 것을 고르시오.

① you – Louise ② big – circle ③ sugar – coffee
④ drive – finish ⑤ large – tall

65 다음 중 품사가 같은 단어끼리 짝지어진 것이 아닌 것을 고르시오.

① about – but ② like – take ③ oops – wow
④ desk – sky ⑤ quickly – heavily

혼동하기 쉬운 품사: 형용사와 부사

[01-03] 다음 중 품사가 다른 하나는?

01 loudly   now   sadly   colorful   safely   inside   _____

02 badly   here   lovely   hardly   happily   perfectly   _____

03 tired   strange   friendly   silly   seriously   quiet   _____

04 다음 중 형용사를 모두 빈칸에 쓰시오.

costly   here   boring   exciting   today   sick   cheap   quick

_____

05 다음 중 부사를 모두 빈칸에 쓰시오.

yesterday   soon   funny   softly   greatly   monthly   heavily   terribly

_____

[06-07] 다음 문장에서 형용사에 모두 밑줄 치시오.

06 A) He bought a small red car.

B) I have an old wooden chair.

07 A) This book is interesting.

B) She wore a long beautiful dress.

[08-09] 다음 문장에서 부사에 모두 밑줄 치시오.

08 A) She sings very well.

B) They arrived late.

09 A) Please speak clearly.

B) He always gets up early.

[10-14] 다음 중 알맞은 단어를 빈칸에 넣으시오.

〈보기〉 We couldn't paly tennis because it was raining **heavily**. (heave / heavily)

10 A) She sings _____. (beautiful / beautifully)

B) The weather is _____ cold today. (extreme / extremely)

C) The dog barked _____. (loud / loudly)

D) She is _____ tired after the trip. (complete / completely)

11 A) The cake tastes _____. (sweet / sweetly)

B) He came _____ for the meeting. (late / lately)

C) The flowers smell _____. (nice / nicely)

D) He is a _____ artist. (great / greatly)

12 A) He drives _____ at night. (careful / carefully)

B) He answered the question _____. (quick / quickly)

C) The children played _____ in the yard. (happy / happily)

D) The news made him feel _____. (sad / sadly)

13 A) The test was _____ easy. (surprising / surprisingly)

B) The cat is _____ sleeping on the sofa. (quiet / quietly)

C) She danced _____ at the party. (beautiful / beautifully)

D) Jack's answer was _____. (correct / correctly)

14 A) The soup tastes _____. (good / well)

B) She was _____ happy with her gift. (real / really)

C) The movie was _____ boring. (terrible / terribly)

D) They walked _____ in the park. (slow / slowly)

정답 p. 109 **실전문제**

[15-19] 다음 밑줄 친 단어가 형용사인지 부사인지 구분하시오.

15 A) The <u>colorful</u> flowers grow in the garden. _____

B) She cooked dinner <u>deliciously</u> for her family. _____

C) He walked <u>fast</u> to catch the bus. _____

D) She <u>peacefully</u> walked along the beach. _____

16 A) Is it <u>really</u> 6:45, or is my watch <u>fast</u>? _____ _____

B) The <u>bright</u> sun shone in the <u>clear</u> blue sky. _____ _____

C) Buying a car can be <u>costly</u>, but it's useful. _____

D) The <u>quiet</u> library was a <u>perfect</u> place to study. _____ _____

*shine: 빛나다

17 A) Ella was very <u>friendly</u>, and I liked her. _____

B) He smiled <u>brightly</u> when he saw his friend. _____

C) He <u>nervously</u> waited for his wife. _____

D) She felt <u>lonely</u> after moving to a new city. _____

18 A) The <u>big</u> dog barked <u>loudly</u> at the boy. _____ _____

B) The <u>main</u> reason for living in Spain is the weather. _____

C) You look <u>lovely</u> in that dress. _____

D) It is a piece of <u>important</u> advice. _____

19 A) She sang <u>gracefully</u> at the concert <u>last</u> night. _____ _____

B) The <u>tall</u> tree provided shade on the hot day. _____

C) The <u>angry</u> customer demanded a refund. _____

D) I like his sister. She's <u>so</u> <u>funny</u>. _____ _____

*provide: 제공하다 *shade: 그늘 *demand: 요구하다 *refund: 환불

20 다음 중 알맞은 단어를 넣으시오. (bad/badly)

A) The weather was so _____ that we had to cancel our picnic.

B) His behavior in class was really _____ today.

C) He sings _____.

D) The dog was _____ injured.

*behavior: 행동

21 다음 중 알맞은 단어를 넣으시오. (hard/hardly)

A) He works _____ every day.

B) She hit the ball _____.

C) She could _____ believe her eyes.

D) I can _____ hear you.

22 다음 중 알맞은 단어를 넣으시오. (high/highly)

A) J. K. Rowling is a _____ successful writer.

B) How _____ is the Eiffel Tower?

C) Choose foods that are _____ in fiber and low in calories.

D) He's a _____ gifted young singer.

*fiber: 섬유   *gifted: 재능이 있는

23 다음 중 알맞은 단어를 넣으시오. (late/lately)

A) She arrived _____ to the concert.

B) I've been feeling tired _____.

C) It was _____ summer when it happened.

D) Have you seen him _____?

24 다음 중 알맞은 단어를 넣으시오. (quick/quickly)

A) She finished her work _____ and left for the day.

B) Do I have time for a _____ shower before we go out?

C) Please reply to the email _____.

D) I took a _____ look at the map.

25 다음 중 밑줄 친 부분에 품사가 다른 하나는?

① The early bird gets the worm.
② Olivia is early today.
③ It is early morning.
④ The garden is pretty in early June.
⑤ She woke up early to catch the first train.

26 다음 중 밑줄 친 부분에 품사가 다른 하나는?

① The car is really fast.
② I like fast runners.
③ That animal is very fast.
④ She runs fast.
⑤ He bought a fast computer.

27 다음 중 밑줄 친 부분에 품사가 다른 하나는?

① He studied hard for the exam.
② She worked hard all day.
③ You need to hit the ball hard.
④ The task was hard to complete.
⑤ Ella was concentrating very hard.

*concentrate: 집중하다

28 다음 중 밑줄 친 부분에 품사가 다른 하나는?

① The bird flew high in the sky.
② The mountain is very high.
③ She has a high position in the company.
④ The prices are too high.
⑤ He jumped over a high fence.

29 다음 중 밑줄 친 부분에 품사가 다른 하나는?

① This is the last piece of cake.
② He was the last person to leave.
③ We met last on Monday.
④ The last chapter of the book is exciting.
⑤ The last train leaves at midnight.

30 다음 중 밑줄 친 부분에 품사가 다른 하나는?

① He arrived late to the party.
② We had a late dinner.
③ The bus came ten minutes late.
④ She often works late.
⑤ They stayed up late.

31 다음 중 밑줄 친 부분에 품사가 다른 하나는?

① She has long hair.
② It's a long journey.
③ The movie was too long.
④ They wrote a long letter.
⑤ He waited long for the bus.

32 다음 중 밑줄 친 부분에 품사가 다른 하나는?

① It's pretty cold today.
② She is pretty.
③ The flowers are pretty.
④ The dress looks pretty on her.
⑤ The sunset is pretty tonight.

33 다음 중 밑줄 친 부분에 품사가 다른 하나는?

① James reads quite well for his age.
② I don't feel very well.
③ She dances well.
④ The team played well.
⑤ The project is going well.

[34-35] 다음 빈칸에 good 또는 well을 넣으시오.

⟨보기⟩ Jack is a **good** worker.

34 A) My new business isn't doing very _____ at the moment.
B) I like your new sweater. It looks _____ on you.
C) Jack plays tennis, but he's not very _____ at it.
D) I didn't sleep _____ last night.

35 A) My exam results were very _____.
B) Harry didn't do _____ in his final exams.
C) The weather was _____ while they were away.
D) Harry cooks _____, making delicious meals that everyone enjoys.

*final exams: 기말고사

[36-37] 괄호 안의 단어를 사용하여 형용사 또는 부사로 빈칸에 넣으시오.

〈보기〉 The little girl smiled **happily**. She had a **happy** face. (happy)

36 A) Liza is _____. She walks _____. (quick)

B) Nancy is a _____ girl. She drives her car _____. (careless)

C) The man is _____. He behaves _____. (nice)

D) He was _____ injured. He had a _____ accident. (bad)

37 A) Rose and Kate can do the math problems _____. They think math is an _____ school subject. (easy)

B) Nicole is a _____ writer. She writes _____. (good)

C) It's a _____ picture. It looks _____. (beautiful)

D) A: You must drive _____ in this road. It is a _____ road. (slow, dangerous)

38 다음 중 어법상 옳은 문장은?

① I make a lot of money. I work very hardly.

② Kate didn't sleep good last night.

③ She spoke soft to the children.

④ He performed poorly in the competition.

⑤ We must make decisions quick.

*competition: 대회, 시합

39 다음 중 어법상 옳은 문장은?

① Don't feel badly about what happened last night.

② I felt extremely unhappy about it.

③ They were happy married for 20 years.

④ He doesn't speak loud.

⑤ Your garden looks beautifully.

40 다음 중 어법상 옳은 문장을 모두 고르시오.

① I was late for work because the bus arrived lately.

② Buying a BMW is costly.

③ He had to stay lately at work to finish the report.

④ They waited long for the train to arrive.

⑤ The chef prepared the meal perfect.

⑥ He is a wonderfully good singer.

⑦ The flowers in the garden smell sweetly.

41 다음 중 어법상 틀린 문장은?

① He quickly finished his homework, so he could go outside and play.

② He could hardly believe his luck when he won the lottery.

③ They had a lovely dinner by the beach.

④ The weather is unusually warm today.

⑤ She feels badly about the mistake.

42 다음 중 어법상 틀린 문장은?

① He is a very well student.

② Have you read any good books lately?

③ She will finish her homework soon.

④ He worked hard to achieve his goals.

⑤ Tim played the piano greatly.

[43-45] 문법적 오류를 모두 찾아 바르게 그치시오.

〈보기〉 She plays basketball competitive.　　competitive → competitively

43 A) I'm doing good.　　_____ → _____

B) The dogs barked at the people angry.　　_____ → _____

C) She drove her car very careful.　　_____ → _____

44 A) Martin practices the violin happy every day.　　_____ → _____

B) Frank exercises hardly to stay in good shape.　　_____ → _____

C) Our team played bad.　　_____ → _____

*stay in good shape: 건강을 유지하다

45 A) Bill was here, but he left sudden.　　_____ → _____

B) They solved the puzzle quick.　　_____ → _____

C) He speaks French very good.　　_____ → _____

실전문제

46 다음 글에서 형용사 5개를 찾아 빈칸에 쓰시오.

> The young boy has a blue bike. He rides it on the wide road every day. The warm sun shines on a quiet park.
>
> *shine: 비추다

_____ _____ _____ _____ _____

47 다음 글에서 형용사 7개를 찾아 빈칸에 쓰시오.

> The little girl has a small dog. They walk together in the green park on a sunny day. The gentle breeze and fresh air make the afternoon perfect.
>
> *breeze: 산들바람

_____ _____ _____ _____ _____

_____ _____

48 다음 글에서 부사 5개를 찾아 빈칸에 쓰시오.

> Anna sings beautifully in the choir. She always arrives early for practice. Her friends speak softly during the songs. After practice, they happily eat snacks.
>
> *choir: 합창단

_____ _____ _____ _____ _____

49 다음 글에서 부사 6개를 찾아 빈칸에 쓰시오.

> Jake loves playing sports. He trains regularly to stay strong. During practice, he runs fast and jumps high. He listens carefully to his coach and plays fairly with his teammates. After the game, he smiles happily.
>
> *train: 훈련하다

_____ _____ _____ _____ _____

_____

50 다음 글에서 형용사 7개와 부사 2개를 찾아 빈칸에 쓰시오.

> Last summer, we visited a beautiful city. The weather was warm and sunny. We walked around the old streets slowly and took many pictures. Our guide spoke clearly and told us interesting stories.

형용사: _____ _____ _____ _____

_____ _____ _____

부사: _____ _____

꼭 알아야 하는 영문법
문장성분과 5형식

● 미리 알고 가기

품사와 문장성분(문장의 구성 요소)의 차이점

품사	문장성분
'ㅇㅇ'사로 명칭 명사, 대명사 동사 형용사, 부사 전치사, 접속사 감탄사	'ㅇㅇ'어로 명칭 주어 서술어(동사) 목적어 보어 수식어(구): 부사(구), 전치사구

	Mike	likes	dogs	and	cats.
품사	명사	동사	명사	접속사	명사
문장성분	주어	동사	목적어		

	I	live	in	Seoul.
품사	대명사	동사	전치사	명사
문장성분	주어	동사	전치사구	

문장성분 > 품사 (문장성분이 품사보다 더 큰 개념이다.)

문장성분이란?

문장성분 (문장의 구성 요소)에는 주어, 동사, 목적어, 보어와 이 요소들을 꾸며주는 수식어(구)가 있다.

01 **주어: 동작을 행하는 주체이며, 우리말 '~은, ~는, ~이, ~가'로 주로 해석된다.
주어가 될 수 있는 품사는 명사, 대명사가 있다.**

  The sun shines. 태양은 빛난다. (The sun: 명사)

  She is a middle school student. 그녀는 중학생이다. (She: 대명사)

02 **동사: 주어의 행동이나 상태를 나타내며, 우리말 '~이다, ~하다'로 주로 해석된다.**

  We **play** baseball there. 우리는 거기서 야구를 한다.

  I **know** the rules of the game. 나는 그 게임의 규칙을 안다.

내용 이해하기

03 목적어: 동사가 의미하는 동작의 대상이 되며, 우리말 '~을, ~를 '로 주로 해석된다.
목적어가 될 수 있는 품사는 주어와 마찬가지로 명사, 대명사가 있다.

I teach **history**. 나는 역사를 가르친다. (history: 명사)

My sister bought **it**. 나의 누나는 그것을 샀다. (it: 대명사)

04 보어: 주어를 보충 설명하면 주격 보어, 목적어를 보충 설명하면 목적격 보어라고 한다.
[주어+동사] 또는 [주어+동사+목적어]로만 의미가 완전하지 않은 문장이 있기 때문에
보어를 사용함으로써 완전한 문장을 이룬다. 보어가 될 수 있는 품사는 명사, 형용사가 있다.

A. 주격 보어

- She became **a doctor**. 그녀는 의사가 되었다. (a doctor: 명사)

  a doctor는 주어 She를 보충 설명하는 주격 보어로 사용되었다.

- I am **happy**. 나는 행복하다. (happy: 형용사)

  주격 보어가 없으면 'I am…'으로만은 의미가 전달되지 않으므로 주격 보어인 happy를 사용해 완전한 문장을 만든다.

B. 목적격 보어

- This movie made him **a star**. 이 영화는 그를 스타로 만들었다 (a star: 명사)

  a star는 목적어 him을 보충 설명하는 목적격 보어로 사용되었다.

- He made me **happy**. 그는 나를 행복하게 했다. (happy: 형용사)

  목적격 보어가 없는 'He made me…' 로만은 의미가 완전히 전달되지 않으므로 목적격 보어인 happy를 사용해 완전한 문장을 만든다.

05 수식어(구): 부사(구), 전치사구 등은 생략해도 문장의 형식에 영향을 주지 않는다.

A. 부사(구): 부사(구)는 동사, 형용사, 부사 등을 수식하는 역할을 한다. 부사구는 when(언제), how(어떻게), where(어디서), why(왜) 등의 질문에 대답하며 문장의 상황이나 동작을 더 자세하게 설명한다.

- She talks **very slowly**. 그녀는 매우 천천히 말한다.

  'very slowly'는 부사구로 how(어떻게)의 질문에 자세히 설명하는 역할을 한다.

- He is **really** smart. 그는 **정말** 똑똑하다.

  really(정말)는 부사이며 형용사 smart(똑똑한)를 꾸며주고 있다.

- She speaks **very** quickly. 그녀는 **매우** 빠르게 말을 한다.

  very(매우)는 부사이며 부사 quickly(빠르게)를 꾸며주고 있다.

B. 전치사구: 전치사구는 전치사와 그 뒤에 오는 명사(구)로 구성되며, 위치, 방향, 시간 등을 나타내는 역할을 한다.

- The book is **on the desk**. 그 책은 책상 위에 있다.

  'on the desk'는 전치사구로 책이 어디에 있는지 위치를 나타낸다.

- We practice football **at 7:00 PM**. 우리는 저녁 7시에 축구 연습을 한다.

  'at 7:00 PM'은 전치사구로 시간을 나타낸다.

내용 이해하기

연습문제   정답 pp. 111-112

[01-10] 밑줄 친 부분의 문장성분을 S(주어), V(동사), C(보어), O(목적어), M(수식어)으로 쓰시오.

01 A) <u>I</u> <u>work</u>.
        S   V

   B) <u>I</u> <u>walk</u> <u>slowly</u>.

   C) <u>Jack</u> <u>is</u> <u>nice</u>.

   D) <u>Children</u> <u>like</u> <u>toys</u>.

02 A) <u>My uncle</u> <u>is</u> <u>a farmer</u>.

   B) <u>I</u> <u>met</u> <u>Sally</u> <u>yesterday</u>.

   C) <u>She</u> <u>is</u> <u>very kind</u>.

   D) <u>I</u> <u>like</u> <u>him</u>.

03 A) <u>We</u> often <u>play</u> <u>tennis and basketball</u>.

   B) <u>Sam</u> <u>read</u> many <u>books</u> <u>last year</u>.

   C) <u>The pasta</u> <u>looks</u> <u>delicious</u>.

   D) <u>The cat</u> <u>was</u> <u>black</u>.

04 A) <u>I</u> <u>agree</u> <u>with you</u>.

   B) <u>The cat</u> <u>is sleeping</u> <u>under the desk</u>.

   C) Don't <u>sit</u> <u>on the floor</u>.

   D) <u>We</u> <u>were</u> <u>late</u> <u>because of the heavy snow</u>.

05 A) <u>I</u> <u>play</u> <u>tennis</u> <u>on Sundays</u>.

   B) <u>The dog</u> <u>feels</u> <u>soft</u> and <u>warm</u>.

   C) <u>You</u> <u>look</u> <u>great</u> <u>today</u>.

   D) <u>They</u> <u>are washing</u> <u>their car</u>.

06 A) <u>My hobby</u> <u>is</u> <u>running</u>.

   B) <u>Jack</u> <u>is</u> <u>good</u> <u>at painting ceilings</u>.

   C) <u>Robin</u> <u>brushes</u> <u>his teeth</u> <u>twice a day</u>.

   D) <u>Ava</u> <u>doesn't work</u> <u>in the morning</u>.

07 A) <u>Henry</u> <u>lost</u> <u>his wallet</u> <u>yesterday</u>.

   B) <u>Isabella</u> <u>bought</u> <u>ice cream</u> <u>for us</u>.

   C) <u>My suit</u> <u>looks</u> <u>perfect</u>.

   D) <u>Always</u> <u>keep</u> <u>calm</u>.

08 A) <u>This novel</u> <u>is</u> <u>really</u> <u>interesting</u>.

   B) <u>He</u> <u>began</u> <u>working</u> <u>at 8:00</u>.

   C) <u>Oliver</u> <u>reads</u> <u>a lot</u>.

   D) <u>Today</u>, <u>I</u> <u>will cook</u> <u>dinner</u>.

정답 p. 112 내용 이해하기

09 A) <u>Derek</u> <u>is</u> a good <u>writer</u>.   B) <u>The train</u> <u>was</u> <u>late</u> <u>because of the accident</u>.

C) <u>Kevin</u> <u>looked</u> <u>nervous</u> <u>before his performance</u>.   D) <u>I</u> will <u>call</u> <u>a taxi</u> <u>for you</u>.

10 A) <u>Listen</u> <u>carefully</u>!   B) <u>This bus</u> doesn't <u>go</u> <u>to London</u>.

C) <u>My brother</u> <u>writes</u> <u>with his left hand</u>.   D) <u>She</u> <u>only</u> <u>eats</u> <u>fish</u>.

문장의 5형식

문장의 5형식	1형식: 주어+동사 2형식: 주어+동사+주격 보어 3형식: 주어+동사+목적어 4형식: 주어+동사+간접 목적어+직접 목적어 5형식: 주어+동사+목적어+목적격 보어

01 1형식: [주어+동사]

A. [주어+동사]만으로 완전한 문장을 이루지만, 문장을 수식해 주는 부사(구)나 전치사구도 올수 있지만 이는 문장의 형식에 영향을 주지 않는다.

- <u>Andy</u> <u>walks</u>. 앤디는 걷는다.
  [주어 + 동사]

- <u>Andy</u> <u>walks</u> <u>slowly</u>. 앤디는 천천히 걷는다.
  [주어 + 동사 + 부사]

- <u>Andy</u> <u>walks</u> <u>very slowly</u>. 앤디는 매우 천천히 걷는다.
  [주어 + 동사 + 부사구]

- <u>Andy</u> <u>walks</u> <u>slowly</u> <u>along the river</u>. 앤디는 강을 따라 천천히 걷는다.
  [주어 + 동사 + 부사 + 전치사구]

B. ⟨There[Here]+be동사+주어~⟩ There나 Here는 형식상 주어 자리에 위치할 뿐, 문장의 주어는 아니며 be동사 다음에 오는 말이 주어이므로 There~ 또는 Here~ 구문은 1형식 문장이다.

- There is **a man** on the roof. 지붕 위에 한 남자가 있어.
- There are **many people** in the park. 공원에 많은 사람들이 있다.
- Here are **the boys**. 여기 그 남자 아이들이 있다.

내용 이해하기

연습문제 (1형식)   정답 p 112

[01-04] 다음 문장에 주어에는 S를, 동사에는 V로 쓰고 밑줄을 그으시오.

01 A) <u>The sun</u> <u>rises</u> in the east.　　　B) They talked too loudly in the library.
　　　　　　S　　V

　　　C) I'm happy.　　　　　　　　　　D) She exercises every morning.

02 A) His dog barks loudly.　　　　　　B) My class starts at 8:00.

　　　C) There is an apple on the table.　　D) We always eat dinner together.

03 A) He likes vegetables.　　　　　　B) I want something to drink.

　　　C) This little black dress is expensive.　D) Those kids speak English.

04 A) There are a lot of people on the street.　B) She took the test last Friday.

　　　C) We talked for hours.　　　　　　D) The little girl likes to play at the playground.

[05-10] 괄호 안의 단어를 사용하여 빈칸을 완성하시오. (필요시 단어 변형)

05 Michael과 나는 도서관에 있다. (library)

　　　Michael and I _____ _____ _____ _____.

06 William은 담배를 너무 많이 핀다. (smoke, too)

　　　William _____ _____ _____.

07 그 전화가 울렸다. (phone, ring)

　　　_____ _____ _____.

08 Isabella는 Boston에 산다. (live)

　　　Isabella _____ _____ _____.

정답 p. 112 **내용 이해하기**

09 많은 사람들이 공항에 있다. (many, airport)

There _____ _____ _____ at _____ _____.

10 나는 11시에 잔다. (at)

I _____ _____ _____.

02 2형식: [주어+동사+주격 보어]

[주어+동사+주격 보어]로 이루어진 문장으로 <be동사/감각동사/상태변화 동사>가 2형식에 쓰인다.
주격 보어는 주어의 상태나 동작을 설명하는 것으로 명사나 형용사가 올 수 있다.

be동사+명사/형용사	Frank **is a farmer**. 프랭크는 농부이다. He **is clever**. 그는 영리하다.
감각동사(feel, look, smell, sound, taste)+형용사	The cat **feels soft** and **warm**. 그 고양이는 부드럽고 따뜻함을 느낀다. You **look great** today. 너 오늘 멋져 보인다.
상태변화 동사(become, get, grow, turn 등)+명사/형용사	Jim **became a pilot**. 짐은 비행기 조종사가 되었다. She **gets tired** easily. 그녀는 쉽게 지친다.

2형식 동사 뒤에는 부사가 올 수 없다.

A. The cat **feels soft** and **warm**. 그 고양이는 부드럽고 따뜻함을 느낀다.
   The cat feels softly and warmly. (✗)
B. You **look great** today. 너 오늘 멋져 보인다.
   You look greatly today. (✗)

감각동사 뒤에 명사(구)가 오면, '~처럼, ~같이'라는 뜻의 전치사가 반드시 필요하다.
'감각동사 + like + 명사(구)' '~처럼 …하다'

It **sounds like a good plan**. 그것은 좋은 계획처럼 들려.
It sounds a good plan. (✗)

연습문제 (2형식) 정답 p. 113

[01-04] 다음 중 문맥에 맞는 단어를 고르시오.

01 A) This fabric feels so (good / well) on the skin.

B) Ethan crossed the street (quick / quickly).

C) The cookies smelled (delicious / deliciously).

D) Even from a distance, Ethan's pace looked (quick / quickly).

E) Helen dances (beautiful / beautifully).

내용 이해하기
정답 p. 113

02 A) The soup tastes (salt / salty).
B) He runs (fast / fastly).
C) I can do it (easy / easily).
D) These flowers smell (wonderful / wonderfully).
E) The coffee tastes (bitter / bitterly) because it was burned.

03 A) The flowers (smell / look) so pretty in the sunlight.
B) The music (sounds / feels) loud and annoying.
C) The lotion (smells / feels) like lavender.
D) The sea (looks / tastes) so refreshing on a hot day.
E) The coffee (smell / tastes / look) strong, just the way I like it.

04 A) John became (happy / happily).
B) The weather turned (terrible / terribly).
C) My business grew (quick / quickly) in the first year.
D) He got (angry / angrily) after listening to her story.
E) The girl smiled (happy / happily).

[05-07] 괄호 안의 단어를 사용하여 빈칸을 완성하시오. (필요시 단어 변형)

05 가을에는 잎들이 갈색으로 변한다. (autumn, turn)

_____ _____, the _____ _____ _____.

06 그녀는 화가 나서 아이들에게 소리를 질렀다. (become, yell at)

_____ _____ _____ and _____ _____ the _____.

07 너 오늘 정말 멋져 보인다! (really)

_____ _____ _____ _____ _____!

[08-10] 다음 문장의 형식을 고르시오.

08 A) We walk to school. (1형식, 2형식)   B) Sam was tired. (1형식, 2형식)
C) My dad is a business man. (1형식, 2형식)   D) The bell rang. (1형식, 2형식)

정답 p. 113 **내용 이해하기**

09 A) Liam is a good student. (1형식, 2형식)   B) I live in Seoul. (1형식, 2형식)
C) The boys look handsome. (1형식, 2형식)   D) Daniel is very busy. (1형식, 2형식)

10 A) Miranda is sick today. (1형식, 2형식)   B) He runs fast. (1형식, 2형식)
C) The weather is terrible. (1형식, 2형식)   D) The blanket feels soft. (1형식, 2형식)

03 3형식: [주어+동사+목적어]

[주어+동사+목적어]로 이루어진 문장으로 일반동사(like, play, want 등)의 목적어를 필요로 하는 문장 구조이다. 목적어로는 명사, 대명사, to부정사, 동명사 등이 올 수 있다.

Andrew likes **dogs**. 앤드류는 개를 좋아한다. (dogs: 명사)

I like **them**, too. 나 역시 그들을 좋아한다. (them: 대명사)

I want **to go** home now. 나는 지금 집에 가고 싶다. (to go: to부정사)

We enjoy **listening** to music. 우리는 음악 듣는 것을 즐긴다. (listening: 동명사)

주의 discuss, marry, mention, enter 등의 동사는 목적어를 반드시 필요로 하는 타동사이므로 전치사 없이 바로 목적어가 와야 한다.

We **discussed** plans for the trip. 우리는 그 여행 계획에 대해 논의했다.
~~We discussed about plans for the trip.~~

He **married** Louise in 2019. 그는 2019년에 루이스랑 결혼했다.
~~He married with Louise in 2019.~~

연습문제 (3형식)   정답 p. 113

[01-03] 다음 문장에 주어에는 S를, 동사에는 V를, 목적어에는 O를 쓰고 밑줄을 그으시오.

01 A) Daniel usually drinks tea in the morning.   B) We parked the car in the parking lot.
      S   V   O

C) My mom loves us very much.   D) She likes writing novels.

02 A) We had a great time at the party.   B) I usually take a shower before going to school.

C) Jack and Ron like to play basketball.   D) Colin enjoys running.

03 A) I opened the box very carefully.   B) Harry practiced the violin every day.

C) I rang the bell a few times.   D) They left a note for Jack.

내용 이해하기

[04-07] 괄호 안의 단어를 사용하여 빈칸을 완성하시오. (필요시 단어 변형)

04 나의 엄마는 매일 집 청소를 하신다. (clean)

_____ _____ _____ _____ _____ _____

05 그녀는 책 읽는 것을 즐긴다. (enjoy)

_____ _____ _____ _____

06 내 친구는 추운 날씨를 싫어한다. (dislike)

_____ _____ _____ _____ _____

07 Sally는 파란 눈을 가졌다.

_____ _____ _____ _____

[08-10] 다음 문장의 형식을 고르시오.

08 A) I got up late this morning. (1형식, 2형식, 3형식)
B) Harry has many friends. (1형식, 2형식, 3형식)
C) The hotel bathroom was very dirty. (1형식, 2형식, 3형식)
D) I usually have breakfast at 7:30. (1형식, 2형식, 3형식)

09 A) They bought a big house. (1형식, 2형식, 3형식)
B) Billy is American. (1형식, 2형식, 3형식)
C) The coffee smells good. (1형식, 2형식, 3형식)
D) Will does all the cleaning. (1형식, 2형식, 3형식)

10 A) Paul has very long hair. (1형식, 2형식, 3형식)
B) I don't know her very well. (1형식, 2형식, 3형식)
C) The book was on the desk. (1형식, 2형식, 3형식)
D) The train stops at Bristol. (1형식, 2형식, 3형식)

04 4형식 : [주어+동사+간접 목적어+직접 목적어]

A. 4형식 수여동사

수여동사는 누군가에게 무엇을 주고받는 것을 표현할 때 사용하며 [주어 + 수여동사 + 간접 목적어 + 직접 목적어]의 문장 구조의 4형식이다. 간접 목적어는 '~에게'로, 직접 목적어는 '~을[를]'로 해석하고 두 개의 목적어를 갖는다.

B. 4형식 : 주어+수여동사+간접 목적어+직접 목적어

주어	동사	간접 목적어 (~에게)	직접 목적어 (~을,~를)
My wife	sent	me	an email.
He	cooked	his mother	a delicious meal.
He	asked	his friends	a few questions.

[주어+동사+간접 목적어+직접 목적어]의 4형식 문장은 [주어+동사+직접 목적어+전치사+간접 목적어]의 3형식 문장으로 바꿔 쓸 수 있다.

C. 3형식: 주어+수여동사+직접 목적어+전치사+간접 목적어

간접 목적어가 뒤로 가는 경우는 3형식이고 동사에 따라 쓰이는 전치사가 다르다.

- to를 사용하는 대표 동사

bring, give, lend, pay, promise read, sell, send, show, take teach, tell, write	+ 사물 목적어(~을,~를) 직접 목적어	+ to +	사람 목적어 (~에게) 간접 목적어

- for를 사용하는 대표 동사

bake, build, buy, cook, do find, get, make, provide	+ 사물 목적어(~을,~를) 직접 목적어	+ for +	사람 목적어 (~에게) 간접 목적어

- of를 사용하는 대표 동사

ask	+ 사물 목적어(~을,~를) 직접 목적어	+ of +	사람 목적어 (~에게) 간접 목적어

주어	동사	직접 목적어 (~에게)	전치사+간접 목적어
My wife	sent	an email	to me.
He	cooked	a delicious meal	for his mother.
He	asked	a few questions	of his friends.

내용 이해하기

D. 4형식을 3형식으로 전환한 문장

- Jack told us a funny story. → Jack told a funny story **to** us. 잭은 우리에게 재미있는 이야기를 했다.

    tell은 수여동사로 'tell+간접 목적어+직접 목적어'의 4형식 구조로 '…에게 ~를 말해주다'라는 의미이다.
    3형식으로 전환할 때는 'tell+사물 목적어+to+사람 목적어'로 바꾸어 쓸 수 있다.

- He bought me flowers. → He bought flowers **for** me. 그는 나에게 꽃을 사주었다.

    buy는 수여동사로 'buy+간접 목적어+직접 목적어'의 4형식 구조로 '…에게 ~를 사주다'라는 의미이다.
    3형식으로 전환할 때는 'buy+사물 목적어+for+사람 목적어'로 바꾸어 쓸 수 있다.

- You have no right to ask me anything. → You have no right to ask anything **of** me.
    당신은 나에게 아무것도 요구할 권리가 없다.

    ask는 수여동사로 'ask+간접 목적어+직접 목적어'의 4형식 구조로 '…에게 ~를 묻다'라는 의미이다.
    3형식으로 전환할 때는 'ask+사물 목적어+ of +사람 목적어'로 바꾸어 쓸 수 있다.

E. 대명사 두 개를 사용하는 경우에는 3형식 형태로 쓴다.

목적어가 모두 대명사일 경우에는 전치사 다음 간접 목적어를 쓴다.

Lend it to him. 이것을 그에게 빌려줘라.
~~Lend him it.~~
대명사 him과 it은 연속해서 사용할 수 없다.

Send it to her. 그녀에게 그것을 보내라.
~~Send her it.~~
대명사 her과 it은 연속해서 사용할 수 없다.

F. 3형식만 가능한 동사

수여의 의미를 갖고 있지만 [간접 목적어 + 직접 목적어] 형태의 4형식 구문을 쓸 수 없는 동사:

describe (묘사하다) donate (기부하다) explain (설명하다)
recommend (추천하다) say (말하다) suggest (제안하다)

Last year he donated $1,000 to the school. 작년에 그는 학교에 천 달러를 기부했다.
~~Last year he donated the school $1,000.~~

Barney said something to me. 바니는 나에게 무언가를 이야기했다.
~~Barney said me something.~~

연습문제 (4형식)

정답 p. 114

[01-03] 다음 문장에 간접 목적어에 IO를, 직접 목적어에 DO를 쓰고 밑줄을 그으시오.

01
A) We asked them a question.
B) I read the baby a book.
C) I wrote my friend a letter.
D) Can you send me a letter?

내용 이해하기 정답 p. 114

02 A) I brought Diane a balloon.   B) The students asked the teacher many questions.

C) Randy threw Robert the football.   D) Give me that book.

03 A) Nicole showed us her photos.   B) Please, pass me the salt.

C) Jack gave Teo and Luna the keys.   D) Mika bought me flowers.

[04-06] 다음 문장의 형식을 고르시오.

04 A) The old man gave the children some money. (3형식, 4형식)

B) My uncle sent me a present. (3형식, 4형식)

C) The students asked the teacher a lot of questions. (3형식, 4형식)

D) I never buy flowers for her. (3형식, 4형식)

05 A) They gave us coffee. (3형식, 4형식)

B) My mother bought me a necklace. (3형식, 4형식)

C) Please buy a new radio for them. (3형식, 4형식)

D) The chef cooked the guests a special meal. (3형식, 4형식)

06 A) I made everyone tea. (3형식, 4형식)

B) I lent Joe my laptop yesterday. (3형식, 4형식)

C) I tried to find a good hotel for my parents. (3형식, 4형식)

D) Ruth showed the photo to us. (3형식, 4형식)

[07-09] 괄호 안의 단어를 사용하여 빈칸을 완성하시오. (필요시 단어 변형)

07 A) I sent Alex a postcard. = I sent a postcard _____ Alex.

B) She bought her friend a present. = She bought a present _____ her friend.

C) You should give Tom a toy. = You should give a toy _____ Tom.

D) She showed all her friends the letter. = She showed the letter _____ all her friends.

08 A) Can you bring the dog some food? = Can you bring some food _____ the dog?
B) I'll cook you dinner. = I'll cook dinner _____ you.
C) We made all the children toys. = We made toys _____ all the children.
D) I asked him a question. = I asked a question _____ him.

09 A) You told me the truth. = You told the truth _____ me.
B) My teacher taught me French. = My teacher taught French _____ me.
C) I found you a pen. = I found a pen _____ you.
D) Can you do me a favor? = Can you do a favor _____ me?

[10-12] 괄호 안의 단어를 사용하여 3형식으로 빈칸을 완성하시오. (필요시 단어 변형)

10 나는 자주 루시에게 이야기(들)를 읽어 준다. (often, story)

_____ _____ read _____ _____ Lucy.

11 이 신문을 Mr. Andrews에게 전달해 주시겠어요? (Could)

_____ you pass _____ _____ _____ Mr. Andrews?

12 Bob은 Ann에게 편지 한 통을 썼다. (write)

Bob _____ _____ _____ _____ Ann.

[13-15] 괄호 안의 단어를 사용하여 4형식으로 빈칸을 완성하시오. (필요시 단어 변형)

13 나는 어제 Peter에게 점심을 주었다. (give)

_____ _____ Peter _____ _____.

14 내가 너한테 내 사진(들) 보여줄까? (show)

Can _____ _____ _____ _____ _____ ?

15 Carol은 아이들에게 수학을 가르친다. (teach, mathematics)

Carol _____ _____ _____.

내용 이해하기

05 5형식: [주어+동사+목적어+목적격 보어]

[주어+동사+목적어+목적격 보어]로 이루어진 문장으로 목적격 보어는 목적어의 상태나 동작을 설명해 준다.

A. 5형식 동사의 문장 구조

S(주어) V(동사) O(목적어) O.C(목적격 보어)

목적격 보어로 취할 수 있는 조건: 명사, 형용사, 원형 부정사, 현재분사, 과거분사, to 부정사

S	V	O	O.C
We 우리는 그를 교장으로 선출했다.	elected	him	principal. **명사**
My boyfriend 남자 친구는 나를 기쁘게 해줬다.	made	me	happy. **형용사**
Daniel 다니엘은 그녀를 울렸다.	made	her	cry. **원형 부정사(동사원형)**
I 나는 네가 춤을 추고 있는 걸 보았다.	saw	you	dancing. **현재분사(-ing)**
She 그녀는 그녀의 옷을 세탁하도록 시킨다.	has	her clothes	washed. **과거분사(-pp)**
Jack 잭은 내가 파티에 가도록 허락했다.	allowed	me	to go to the party. **to 부정사**

사역이란 의미는 '누군가에게 일을 시키다'라는 의미이고 영어로는 causative verb라 하여 어떤 결과의 원인을 일으킨다는 의미이다.

B. 사역동사 (make/ let/ have)

make, let, have + 목적어+ 원형 부정사

- make + 목적어 + 원형 부정사

사역동사로 쓰인 make는 '~을 강제로 시키다'의 의미이다.

Mom **made dad mow** the lawn. (forced) 엄마는 아빠에게 잔디를 깎게 했다.

~~Mom made dad to mow the lawn. Mom made dad mowing the lawn.~~

- let + 목적어 + 원형 부정사

사역동사로 쓰인 let은 '~을 하도록 허락하다'의 의미이다.

My dad **let me go** to the park by myself. (gave permission) 아빠는 나 혼자 공원에 가게 해 주셨다.

~~My dad let me to go to the park by myself.~~

~~My dad let me going to the park by myself.~~

- have + 목적어 + 원형 부정사

사역동사로 쓰인 have는 '~을 하도록 요청하다'의 의미이다.

Mr. Jackson **had the students do** the homework. (requested/ asked) Jackson선생님은 학생들에게 숙제를 시켰다.

내용 이해하기

C. 준사역 동사 (get/ help)

- get + 목적어 + to 부정사

위의 구문에서의 get은 사역 동사로 스스로 행하지 않고 타인(또는 사물)에게 행위나 동작을 하게 만든다는 의미이다.

She **got me to wash** the dishes. (convinced/ persuaded) 그녀는 나에게 설거지를 시켰다.

- get/have + 목적어 + pp

위의 구문은 타인으로 하여금 어떤 대상에게 어떤 행위나 동작을 하게 만든다는 의미이다.

She **got her watch repaired**. 그녀는 자신의 손목시계를 (누군가를 시켜) 수리했다.
I **have my shirts ironed** every week. 나는 매주 나의 셔츠를 다림질시킨다.

- help + 목적어 + (to) + 원형 부정사

help는 '(목적어)가 ...하도록 돕다'는 의미로 사용된다.

Roberto **helped me (to) improve** my English. (aided) Roberto는 나의 영어실력을 향상시키는데 도움을 주었다.
~~Roberto helped me improving my English.~~
~~Roberto helped me improved my English.~~

다음 두 예문의 차이는?

A) I cut my hair. 나 머리 (직접) 잘랐어.
B) I **had** my hair **cut**. (누군가를 시켜) 머리 잘랐어.

A) I iron my shirts every week. 나는 내가 셔츠를 매주 다린다.
B) I **have** my shirts **ironed** every week. 나는 매주 (누군가를 시켜) 셔츠를 다린다.

D. 지각 동사

지각 동사란 외부에서 받은 자극을 느껴 뇌에서 그 자극을 이해한다는 의미이다.

- 지각 동사는 5가지로 나뉘어져

1. 눈으로 보고   look at / observe / see / watch
2. 귀로 듣고   hear / listen to
3. 코로 냄새 맡으며   smell
4. 혀로 맛을 느끼고   taste
5. 피부로 촉감을 느낀다.   feel / touch

* notice와 sense도 지각 동사이지만 일반적인 감각을 나타내며, 여러 감각(보고, 듣고, 피부로 느낌 등)을 포함할 수 있으며 특정 감각기관에 국한되지 않는다.

- 지각 동사의 문장 구조

S + 지각 동사 + 목적어 + 원형 부정사 / 현재분사(-ing) / 과거분사(-pp)

1. S + 지각 동사 + 목적어 + 원형 부정사

    I **saw Jason dance**. 나는 Jason이 (처음부터 끝까지) 춤을 추는 것을 봤다.
    I **watched the children play**. 나는 그 아이들이 (처음부터 끝까지) 노는 것을 봤다.

2. S + 지각 동사 + 목적어 + 현재분사(-ing)

   I **saw Jason dancing**. 나는 Jason이 (일부만) 춤을 추는 것을 봤다.
   I **watched the children playing**. 나는 그 아이들이 노는 것을 (일부만) 봤다.

   위의 1번 예시처럼 원형 부정사를 쓰는 경우와 2번 예시의 현재 분사(-ing)를 쓰는 경우는 의미 차이가 있다. 〈지각 동사 + 목적어 + 원형 부정사〉가 오면 어떤 사건이나 행위를 처음부터 보거나 듣는다는 의미이고, 현재 분사(-ing)가 오면 한창 진행되고 있는 어떤 사건이나 행위를 보거나 듣는 것을 의미한다.

3. S + 지각 동사 + 목적어 + 과거분사(-pp)

   I **saw him surrounded** by a lot of people. 나는 그가 많은 사람에게 둘러 쌓인 것을 보았다.
   We **heard your name called**. 우리는 너의 이름이 불리우는 것을 들었다.

   〈지각 동사 + 목적어 + 과거 분사(-pp)〉 구문은 목적어가 어떤 상태가 되게 만든다는 의미로 과거 분사는 수동의 의미를 나타낸다.

E. to 부정사를 목적격 보어로 취하는 5형식 동사

S + 동사 + 목적어 + to 원형 부정사
많은 동사들은 〈S + 동사 + 목적어 + to 원형 부정사〉 형태를 취한다.

I advised **him to study** for the exam. 나는 그에게 시험 공부를 하라고 조언했다.
They expected **us to arrive** early. 그들은 우리가 일찍 도착할 것으로 예상했다.
I want **you to listen**. 내 말 좀 들어봐.

advise	충고하다	allow	허락하다	ask	요청하다
cause	원인을 일으키다	enable	가능하게 하다	encourage	장려하다
expect	기대하다	force	강요하다	need	필요하다
order	명령하다	persuade	설득하다	require	요구하다
tell	말하다	want	원하다	warn	경고하다
wish	바라다	would like	하고 싶어하다		

위의 동사는 5형식 동사이면서 3형식(주어+동사+목적어) 동사로도 쓰인다.

F. 3형식과 5형식으로 쓰이는 동사

- 3형식 (S + want + 목적어)

   I **want the cake**. 나는 케익을 원해.
   I **want to eat the cake**. 나는 케익 먹고 싶어.

- 5형식 (S + want + 목적어 + to 부정사)

   I **want you to eat the cake**. 나는 네가 케익을 먹었으면 해.

- 3형식 (S + persuade + 목적어)

   I didn't want to go, but **my friends persuaded me** into it. 나는 가고 싶지 않았지만 친구들이 설득해서 가게 했다.

   전치사구는 목적어가 아니라 형용사구나 부사구의 역할을 한다.

내용 이해하기

- 5형식 (S + persuade + 목적어 + to 부정사)

  I **persuaded her to change her mind**. 나는 그녀를 설득해서 마음을 바꾸게 했다.

- 3형식 (S + make + 목적어)

  Diane **made her own clothes** 다이앤은 자신의 옷을 만들었다.

- 5형식 (S + make + 목적어 + 원형 부정사)

  My parents always **make me do my homework** before I go out.
  우리 부모님은 내가 외출하기 전에 항상 숙제를 시키신다.

- 5형식 (S + make + 목적어 + 과거 분사 (-pp))

  He **made the report written** by his assistant. 그는 조수에게 보고서를 쓰게 했다.

주의 1 일부 동사들은 5형식 〈주어+동사+목적어+to 원형 부정사〉와 3형식 〈주어+동사+ that절〉을 모두 사용할 수 있지만, 어떤 동사들은 5형식 〈주어+동사+목적어+to 원형 부정사〉의 구조만 사용할 수 있다.

1. 〈주어+동사+목적어+to 원형 부정사〉와 〈주어+동사+ that절〉 둘 다 가능한 동사:
   advise, ask, expect, require, tell, warn, wish 등

   5형식: 〈주어+동사+목적어+to 원형 부정사〉
     They advised **us to leave** early. 그들은 우리에게 일찍 가라고 조언했다.

   3형식: 〈주어+동사+ that절〉
     They advised **that** we should leave early. 그들은 우리에게 일찍 떠나는 것이 좋겠다고 조언했다.

   5형식: 〈주어+동사+목적어+to 원형 부정사〉
     I expect **her to arrive** soon. 나는 그녀가 곧 도착할 것으로 기대한다.

   3형식: 〈주어+동사+ that절〉
     I expect **that** she will arrive soon. 나는 그녀가 곧 도착할 것으로 기대한다.

2. 접속사 that을 사용하지 못하고, 5형식 〈주어+동사+목적어+to 원형 부정사〉만 가능한 동사들:
   allow, cause, enable, encourage, force, need, order, persuade, want, would like 등

   Her parents encouraged **her to participate** in the competition.
   그녀의 부모님은 그녀에게 대회에 참가하라고 장려했다.
   ~~Her parents encouraged that she should participate in the competition.~~

   I want **you to study** harder. 나는 네가 더 열심히 공부했으면 좋겠어.
   ~~I want that you study harder.~~

주의 2 'I found it easily.' 와 'I found it easy.'의 차이점은?

문장	형식	의미	설명
I found it **easily**.	3형식	나는 그것을 쉽게 찾았다.	'easily'는 부사로 동사 'found'를 수식한다.
I found it **easy**.	5형식	나는 그것이 쉽다고 느꼈다.	'easy'는 형용사로 목적어 'it'의 상태를 설명한다.

내용 이해하기

연습문제 (5형식)   정답 pp. 114-115

[01-03] 다음 문장에 목적어에 O를, 목적격 보어에 OC를 쓰고 밑줄을 그으시오.

01 A) The noise drove <u>him</u> <u>mad</u>.　　　　B) He painted the wall green.
　　　　　　　　　　O　　OC
　　C) My sister named the dog Boss.　　D) You make me want to cry.

02 A) We consider the matter important.　　B) Listening to this song always makes me happy.

　　C) Now, I call Minnesota home.　　D) I found that class a challenge.

03 A) We call it friendship.　　B) My parents wouldn't allow me to go to the party.

　　C) Danny believes us honest.　　D) I saw you dancing.

[04-07] 다음 문장의 형식을 고르시오.

04 A) My sister made Mary a doll. (3형식, 4형식, 5형식)
　　B) Canada has many beautiful mountains. (3형식, 4형식, 5형식)
　　C) I found his advice very helpful. (3형식, 4형식, 5형식)
　　D) Tom found the book easily. (3형식, 4형식, 5형식)

05 A) I bought a lot of food at the market. (3형식, 4형식, 5형식)
　　B) I called him a fool. (3형식, 4형식, 5형식)
　　C) I made her laugh. (3형식, 4형식, 5형식)
　　D) We let her play outside. (3형식, 4형식, 5형식)

06 A) We chose him our leader. (3형식, 4형식, 5형식)

B) I think him smart. (3형식, 4형식, 5형식)

C) I took some pictures. (3형식, 4형식, 5형식)

D) Cathy sent Henry a novel. (3형식, 4형식, 5형식)

07 A) He got a new job at another university. (3형식, 4형식, 5형식)

B) I ordered him to start early. (3형식, 4형식, 5형식)

C) Tom saw me at the party. (3형식, 4형식, 5형식)

D) Mary told me to go there. (3형식, 4형식, 5형식)

[08-10] 다음 중 올바른 것을 고르시오.

08 A) I asked Sue (lend, to lend, lending) me some money.

B) We heard Jane (played, playing) the piano.

C) I didn't expect you (be, to be, being) here.

D) Mom had me (wash, to wash, washing) the car.

09 A) James advised me (call, to call, calling) you.

B) The boss had his secretary (to send, send) the invitations.

C) My teacher (made, watched, helped) us cleaning the classroom.

D) I will (see, watch, help) them to draw a picture on the ground.

10 A) Please let me (know, to know, knowing) if you finish the work.

B) I felt the ground (shook, shaking).

C) We saw the boys (to cross, crossing, crossed) the street.

D) I observed him (to sing, singing, sang) a song.

[11-15] 괄호 안의 단어를 사용하여 5형식으로 빈칸을 완성하시오. (필요시 단어 변형)

11 나는 네가 행복하기를 원해. (want, be)

_____ _____ _____ _____ _____ happy.

12 Nicole은 나에게 그녀(Nicole)를 위해 기다리라고 말했다. (tell, wait)

Nicole _____ _____ _____ _____ _____ her.

13 Harry는 나를 웃게 만든다. (laugh)

_____ _____ _____ _____ .

14 나는 몇 분 전에 그가 나가는 것 봤다. (see, leave, few)

_____ _____ him _____ a _____ _____ ago.

15 Liam은 그녀에게 그의 시계를 고치도록 시켰다. (get, fix)

Liam _____ her _____ _____ _____ _____ .

1 & 2형식

정답 p. 115 **실전문제**

[01-04] 괄호 안에서 어법상 알맞은 것을 선택 후, 문장의 형식을 쓰시오.

01 A) I don't feel (comfortable / comfortably). _____
B) I was sitting (comfortable / comfortably) in the lounge. _____
C) It is raining (heavy / heavily). _____
D) This table is too (heavy / heavily). _____

02 A) The girl seemed very (polite / politely). _____
B) Ann speaks (polite / politely). _____
C) We arrived there (safe / safely). _____
D) She doesn't feel (safe / safely) in the house on her own. _____

03 A) Michelle smiled (happy / happily). _____
B) John will be so (happy / happily) to see you. _____
C) My team played very (good / well) today. _____
D) Simon doesn't work (good / well) under pressure. _____

04 A) The economy grew (slow / slowly). _____
B) His story is (true / truth). _____
C) The hotel was absolutely (terrible / terribly). _____
D) The team played (terrible / terribly). _____

05 다음 중 빈칸에 들어갈 말로 알맞지 않은 것은?

The new student looks _____.

① kind ② friendly ③ like my best friend
④ unhappy ⑤ politely

06 다음 중 빈칸에 들어갈 말로 알맞지 않은 것은?

The salesperson looks _____.

① lovely ② happiness ③ worried
④ tired ⑤ friendly

1 & 2형식

07 다음 중 문장의 빈칸 (A), (B), (C)에 들어갈 말로 적절한 것은?

- Tom looks very (A) _____.
- The music sounds too (B) _____ in the restaurant.
- You look (C) _____ today. Is everything all right?

① (A) health   (B) loud   (C) well
② (A) health   (B) loudly   (C) unwell
③ (A) healthy   (B) loudly   (C) good
④ (A) healthy   (B) loud   (C) unwell
⑤ (A) healthy   (B) loudly   (C) unwell

08 다음 중 문장의 빈칸 (A), (B), (C)에 들어갈 말로 적절한 것은?

- These flowers (A) _____ roses.
- The food is (B) _____.
- The fireworks (C) _____ so colorful in the night sky.

① (A) smell like   (B) spice   (C) looks
② (A) smells like   (B) spice   (C) look
③ (A) smell like   (B) spicy   (C) look
④ (A) smell   (B) spicy   (C) looks
⑤ (A) smell   (B) spice   (C) look

09 다음 대화를 읽고 빈칸에 들어갈 단어가 알맞게 짝지어진 것은?

Helen: Nicole, have you seen the new dress I bought yesterday?
Nicole: Yes, I have. It **(A)** _____ amazing on you!
Helen: Thanks, but I'm not sure about the color. What do you think?
Nicole: Honestly, it looks a little dull to me.
Helen: Really? I thought it looked **(B)** _____ and **(C)** _____.

* dull: 우중충한

① (A) looks   (B) brightly   (C) cheerful
② (A) looks   (B) bright   (C) cheerful
③ (A) looks   (B) bright   (C) cheerfully
④ (A) look   (B) brightly   (C) cheerful
⑤ (A) look   (B) bright   (C) cheerfully

1 & 2형식

[10-12] 다음 문장에서 어법상 어색한 부분을 찾아 바르게 고쳐 쓰시오. 오류가 없으면 X로 표시하시오.

10 A) The flowers smell well. _____ → _____
B) The stew smells greatly. _____ → _____
C) The soft music makes me feel calmly and relaxed. _____ → _____

*stew: 스튜 (고기와 채소를 넣고 국물이 좀 있게 해서 천천히 끓인 요리)

11 A) His new sweater feels softly. _____ → _____
B) Your new car looks modern. _____ → _____
C) The pie tastes deliciously. _____ → _____

12 A) She looks tire after a long day. _____ → _____
B) The music sounds loudly and exciting. _____ → _____
C) The city sounds differently at night than it does during the day. _____ → _____

13 다음 중 어법상 옳은 것은?

① The cake tastes sweetly.
② The sunset over the ocean was absolutely love.
③ The soup was too salt.
④ The ocean looks calm and peaceful in the evening.
⑤ My new shoes are comfortably.

14 다음 중 어법상 옳은 것은?

① The leaves turn goldenly in fall.
② The sunrise looks amazing over the ocean.
③ The bread is freshly.
④ Your sister became happily.
⑤ The chicken tastes greatly with barbecue sauce.

15 다음 중 어법상 옳은 것을 모두 고르시오.

① The music sounds terrible.
② The weather feels warmly.
③ The flowers look love.
④ The fabric feels soft.
⑤ The shampoo smells nicely.
⑥ The wind feels cool on my face.
⑦ The boys kept quietly.
⑧ It smells really fresh.

1 & 2형식

16 다음 중 어법상 옳은 것을 모두 고르시오.

① The sky turned dark suddenly.
② This blanket is softly.
③ She looks cute with her new haircut.
④ The chocolate cake tastes rich and moisture.
⑤ In October, the leaves turn orange and yellow.
⑥ The apple tastes sweet and juicy.
⑦ The machine sounds loudly.
⑧ The flowers look bright and color in the garden.

17 다음 중 어법상 어색한 문장은?

① People were growing impatient.
② The coffee tastes very good with cream.
③ It gets cold in the mountains at night.
④ The food smells like spicy.
⑤ The house smells like freshly baked cookies.

18 다음 중 어법상 어색한 문장은? (정답 2개)

① The music sounded very joyfully in the concert hall.
② Emma got angry when she heard the news.
③ The flowers smell roses in the garden.
④ She looks happy with her new job.
⑤ The air feels cold at the top of the mountain.

19 다음 중 어법상 어색한 문장을 모두 고르시오.

① The sky looks beautiful when the sun goes down.
② She feels like a queen in her new dress.
③ The pillow feels soft and comfortable.
④ That instrument sounds like a trumpet.
⑤ The steak feels tender and juice.
⑥ You didn't look like well.
⑦ The ice cream tastes cream.
⑧ He spoke quickly.

20 다음 중 어법상 어색한 문장을 모두 고르시오.

① When did you first want to become a teacher?
② The water tastes like salty.
③ She feels badly almost every morning.
④ He smells well.
⑤ The water feels like ice in the winter.
⑥ The music sounds horribly.
⑦ The birds sing happy.
⑧ The sunset looks like a painting.

1 & 2형식: 문장으로 영작 실력 다지기

[21-35] 괄호 안의 단어를 사용하여 빈칸을 완성한 후 몇 형식인지 고르시오. (필요시 단어 변형)

21 가브리엘은 브라질에서 온 학생입니다. (Gabriel, from)

_____ _____ _____ _____
_____ (1형식, 2형식)

22 태양은 동쪽에서 뜬다. (rise, in)

_____ _____ _____ _____
_____ (1형식, 2형식)

23 올림픽은 그리스에서 시작되었다. (The Olympic Games)

_____ _____ _____ _____
_____ (1형식, 2형식)

24 마틴 루터 킹은 용감한 사람이었다. (Martin Luther King)

_____ _____ _____ _____
_____ (1형식, 2형식)

25 마리 퀴리는 훌륭하고 똑똑한 과학자였다. (Marie Curie, great)

_____ _____ _____ _____
_____ _____ (1형식, 2형식)

26 바구니 안에 강아지 한 마리가 있다. (there, basket)

_____ _____ _____ _____
_____ _____ (1형식, 2형식)

1 & 2형식: 문장으로 영작 실력 다지기

정답 p. 116-117 **실전문제**

27 넬슨 만델라는 첫 흑인 대통령이 되었다. (Nelson Mandela, president)

_____ _____ _____ _____ _____
_____ (1형식, 2형식)

28 러시아는 지구에서 가장 큰 나라이다. (Russia, large, country, on)

_____ _____ _____ _____ _____
_____ (1형식, 2형식)

29 그 나뭇잎들은 빨갛고 노랗게 변했다. (leaves, turn)

_____ _____ _____ _____ _____
_____ (1형식, 2형식)

30 케이팝은 많은 나라에서 인기가 있다. (K-pop, popular, country)

_____ _____ _____ _____ _____
_____ (1형식, 2형식)

31 이 음식은 신선하고 건강해 보인다. (fresh)

_____ _____ _____ _____
_____ (1형식, 2형식)

32 크리스는 그의 사무실에서 일하고 있다. (Chris, at)

_____ _____ _____ _____ _____
_____ (1형식, 2형식)

1 & 2형식: 문장으로 영작 실력 다지기

정답 p. 117 **실전문제**

33 키아라는 음악을 듣고 있다. (Kiara, to)

_____ _____ _____ _____ _____

(1형식, 2형식)

34 파리는 에펠탑으로 유명하다. (Paris, Eiffel Tower)

_____ _____ _____ _____ _____

_____ _____ (1형식, 2형식)

35 패트릭은 불평을 너무 많이 한다. (Patrick, complain, too)

_____ _____ _____ _____ _____

(1형식, 2형식)

3 & 4형식

[01-02] 다음 단어를 재구성하여 문장을 완성하시오.

01 A) to/ will/ John/ bring/ a/ cake/ us/ . _____

　　 B) English / us/ teaches/ Mr. Jackson / to/ . _____

02 A) pizza/ us/ made/ Sam/ some/ for/ . _____

　　 B) you/ me/ to/ new/ teach/ a/ can/ song/ ? _____

[03-05] 다음 문장에서 어법상 어색한 부분을 찾아 바르게 고쳐 쓰시오. 오류가 없으면 ✗로 표시하시오.

03 A) Mike married with Karen. _____ → _____

　　 B) He got her for a concert ticket. _____ → _____

　　 C) He lent me some money. _____ → _____

04 A) Please bring some water for me. _____ → _____

　　 B) He mentioned about a book he'd read. _____ → _____

　　 C) She discussed about the idea with her parents. _____ → _____

05 A) Please, don't talk about him anymore. _____ → _____

　　 B) I will explain you the problem. _____ → _____

　　 C) He sent a postcard me. _____ → _____

06 다음 중 빈칸에 들어갈 단어가 다른 하나는?

　　① They baked bread _____ me.　　② I found a pen _____ you.

　　③ He made a cake _____ his wife.　　④ They sent Christmas cards _____ all their customers.

　　⑤ They made sandwiches _____ me.

07 다음 중 빈칸에 들어갈 단어가 다른 하나는?

　　① We made cookies _____ all the children.　　② Could you lend some money _____ me?

　　③ Bring them _____ her.　　④ Read it _____ him.

　　⑤ He gave a gift _____ me.

3 & 4형식 실전문제

08 다음 중 빈칸에 들어갈 단어가 다른 하나는?

① He showed his car _____ me.
② My brother prepares the table _____ us.
③ My brother is building a sand-castle _____ the kids.
④ Laura bought a new dress _____ her mother.
⑤ I will cook a meal _____ you.

09 다음 중 빈칸에 들어갈 단어가 다른 하나는?

① Pass it _____ me, please.
② June asked many questions _____ her sister.
③ We sold goods _____ them.
④ Show your picture _____ Grandpa.
⑤ I took the report _____ Mr. Black.

10 다음 중 빈칸에 들어갈 단어가 다른 하나는?

① Read the email _____ me, will you?
② He teaches German _____ students.
③ They sent the bill _____ me.
④ I made a handmade card _____ my wife.
⑤ The company promised improvements _____ its customers.

*improvement: 개선, 향상

11 다음 중 빈칸에 들어갈 단어가 다른 하나는?

① He wrote a letter _____ them.
② My teacher taught French _____ me.
③ He sold a monitor _____ Andy.
④ He lent his dictionary _____ me.
⑤ Don will do it _____ you.

12 다음 중 빈칸에 들어갈 말로 알맞은 것은?

Would you _____ a glass of wine for me?

① get   ② send   ③ give   ④ sell   ⑤ bring

13 다음 중 빈칸에 들어갈 말로 알맞은 것은?

Jenny will _____ some cookies for us.

① send   ② give   ③ bake   ④ sell   ⑤ teach

3 & 4형식

14 다음 중 빈칸에 들어갈 말로 알맞은 것은?

Nick _____ some flowers for her.

① gave ② sent ③ bought ④ brought ⑤ showed

15 다음 중 빈칸에 들어갈 말로 어법상 어색한 것을 모두 고르시오.

They _____ a book to me.

① gave ② sent ③ bought ④ brought ⑤ read

16 다음 중 빈칸에 들어갈 말로 어법상 어색한 것을 모두 고르시오.

They _____ a new TV for my brother.

① gave ② sent ③ bought ④ brought ⑤ showed

17 다음 중 어법상 올바른 문장은?

① She lent me to some money.
② Mom gave a toy me.
③ Miss Green asked some questions for me.
④ My brother cooked me some soup.
⑤ Bille sent us for a Christmas card.

18 다음 중 어법상 올바른 문장은? (정답 2개)

① He wrote her to a letter.
② You sold it to me.
③ His sister gave me it.
④ She explained me the problem.
⑤ I said it to them.

19 다음 중 어법상 올바른 문장을 모두 고르시오.

① I sent the package me.
② I will get it to you.
③ The king built a palace for the queen.
④ Clara showed me the picture of her parents.
⑤ The boy asked to me what the problem was.

3 & 4형식

20 다음 중 어법상 어색한 것은? (정답 2개)

① Please explain your decision to us.
② Can you suggest me a good pet shop?
③ She lent it to Bob.
④ She described the situation to us.
⑤ Mrs. Willson gave us it.

21 다음 중 어법상 어색한 것은? (정답 2개)

① Andy showed her photos for me.
② They will do that for me.
③ The boy gave a pebble to the girl.
④ Can you bring a cup of coffee for us?
⑤ Mom will buy me books on Indonesia.

*pebble: 조약돌

22 다음 중 어법상 어색한 것은? (정답 2개)

① He said me something.
② Can you find me for a job?
③ I told the problem to Sam.
④ Will you send me the package?
⑤ I recommend this book to my students.

23 다음 보기 문장과 형식이 같은 것은? (정답 2개)

〈보기〉 He made us some cookies.

① He made a wooden chair for his daughter.
② I found the key for her.
③ We did it for them.
④ He sent Mina a gift card.
⑤ Sally taught me the importance of teamwork.

24 다음 보기 문장과 형식이 같은 것은?

〈보기〉 Bill writes letters to me every week.

① Aron gave his sister a book.
② Show Jack your magic.
③ Take John your notes.
④ She will make us a delicious meal.
⑤ She sold her house to the Simpsons.

3 & 4형식

25 다음 문장 중 우리말을 영어로 바르게 옮긴 것을 모두 고르시오.

① 그는 그의 친구에게 영화 표 2장을 주었다. He gave his friends two movie tickets.
② 그는 나에게 그것을 보냈다. He sent me it.
③ 그는 나에게 피자 한판을 사줬다. He bought a pizza to me.
④ 그는 그녀에게 몇가지 질문을 했다. He asked her a few questions.
⑤ 그는 그녀에게 종이 비행기를 만들어 줬다. He made a paper airplane to her.

26 다음 문장 중 우리말을 영어로 바르게 옮긴 것을 모두 고르시오.

① 나에게 그 서류를 가져와 주세요. Bring me the document, please.
② 삼촌은 나에게 사진 한 장을 보여주셨다. My uncle showed me a photo.
③ 엄마는 나에게 과자를 몇 개 만들어 주셨다. My mom made some cookies for me.
④ 그 경찰관은 나의 지갑을 찾아 주었다. The police officer found my wallet to me.
⑤ 제게 만원만 빌려주실 수 있나요? Can you lend ₩10,000 for me?

27 다음 문장 중 우리말을 영어로 바르게 옮긴 것을 모두 고르시오.

① 아델은 나에게 그 이야기를 하고 있다. Adel is telling the story for me.
② 그는 많은 질문을 나에게 했다. He asked to me many questions.
③ 마이클은 우리에게 영어를 가르치신다. Michael teaches us for English.
④ 해리는 그의 아내에게 강아지 한 마리를 가져다 줬다. Harry brought a dog to his wife.
⑤ 소라는 우리를 위해 간식을 만든다. Sora makes us for snacks.

28 다음 문장 중 우리말을 영어로 바르게 옮긴 것을 모두 고르시오.

① 제시카는 나에게 그녀의 치마를 팔았다. Jessica sold her skirt for me.
② 케빈은 톰에게 생일 선물 하나를 사 주었다. Kevin bought Tom for a birthday present.
③ 부탁 하나만 해도 되나요? Can you do me a favor?
④ 그는 내 필통을 나에게 찾아 주었다. He found my pencil case for me.
⑤ 나의 할아버지 할머니는 나에게 책을 많이 읽어 주신다. My grandparents read many books to me.

3 & 4형식

정답 p. 118 **실전문제**

29 다음 중 문장의 전환이 어법상 바른 것은?

① Could you bring me some water? → Could you bring some water for me?

② Should we cook them dinner? → Should we cook dinner to them?

③ He told me the news. → He told the news of me.

④ I've bought you a gift. → I've bought a gift to you.

⑤ Let's write John a letter in California. → Let's write a letter to John in California.

30 다음 중 문장의 전환이 어법상 바른 것을 모두 고르시오.

① I gave my mother some flowers. → I gave some flowers to my mother.

② He built his parents a house. → He built a house to his parents.

③ I'll send you the report tomorrow. → I'll send the report for you tomorrow.

④ Let me make you some coffee. → Let me make some coffee for you.

⑤ He wants to sell me his old car. → He wants to sell his old car to me.

31 다음 중 문장의 전환이 어법상 바른 것을 모두 고르시오.

① She baked Teo and Noah some cookies. → She baked some cookies for Teo and Noah.

② Sam brought you some flowers. → Sam brought some flowers to you.

③ Can you please pass me the salt? → Can you please pass the salt to me?

④ My brother promised me a laptop. → My brother promised a laptop for me.

⑤ You told me the truth. → You told the truth to me.

32 다음 중 문장의 전환이 어법상 바른 것을 모두 고르시오.

① We gave them some candy. → We gave some candy to them.

② Barbara made him some tea. → Barbara made some tea to him.

③ He sold the family the house. → He sold the house for the family.

④ He paid him $5 to cut the grass. → He paid $5 for him to cut the grass.

⑤ The company built the city a new bridge. → The company built a new bridge for the city.

[33-36] 아래 4형식 문장을 3형식으로 전환하시오.

33 A) She bought her daughter a house. _____

B) He lent her some money. _____

C) We gave them some money. _____

3 & 4형식

34 A) They built their children a tree-house. _____

B) Can you bring me the newspaper? _____

C) Can you get me my hat? _____

35 A) They promised me many things. _____

B) Mom read me a story. _____

C) Let's take her some flowers. _____

36 A) I'll tell you the truth. _____

B) He showed me the photo. _____

C) We bought Jane a present. _____

[37-40] 아래 3형식 문장을 4형식으로 전환하시오.

37 A) Can you teach a new song to me? _____

B) He wrote a poem to me. _____

C) Can you bring some water to her? _____

38 A) She asked a question of me. _____

B) He taught English to them. _____

C) We bought a computer for the boy. _____

39 A) We cooked spaghetti for the children. _____

B) Dave showed his photos to him. _____

C) Jack told the story to me. _____

40 A) Kate found the lost wallet for me. _____

B) He did a favor for James. _____

C) Her dad told something important to her. _____

3형식 : 문장으로 영작 실력 다지기

정답 p. 119 **실전문제**

[41-50] 괄호 안의 단어를 사용하여 빈칸을 완성하시오. (필요시 단어 변형)

41 빌은 채소를 좋아하지 않는다. (vegetable)

_____ _____ _____ _____ _____

42 나는 지난달에 팔이 부러졌다. (break, arm)

_____ _____ _____ _____ _____
_____

43 그녀는 귀에 귀걸이를 하고 있어. (have, on her)

_____ h_____ h_____ e_____ _____
_____ _____

44 그는 아침에 커피를 마신다. (morning)

_____ _____ _____ _____ _____
_____

45 우리는 야생 동물에게 먹이를 주면 안된다. (shouldn't, wild)

_____ _____ _____ _____ _____

3형식 : 문장으로 영작 실력 다지기

정답 p. 119 **실전문제**

46 너 시험 잘 봤어? (pass, test)

_____ _____ _____ _____ ?

47 짐은 일본어를 배우고 있는 중이다. (Jim, learn)

_____ _____ _____ _____ .

48 베토벤은 많은 유명한 음악 작품들을 썼다. (Beethoven, many, piece, of)

_____ _____ _____ _____ _____
_____ _____ .

49 알렉산더 그레이엄 벨은 전화기를 발명했어. (invent)

Alexander Graham Bell _____ _____ _____ .

50 우리는 호텔에서 바다를 볼 수 있었다. (ocean, from)

_____ _____ _____ _____ _____
_____ _____ .

3 & 4형식 : 문장으로 영작 실력 다지기

정답 p. 119

[51-60] 〈보기〉와 같이 주어진 단어를 활용하여 3형식과 4형식으로 영작하시오.

〈보기〉 Eric은 나에게 크리스마스 엽서를 보냈다. (send)

3형식: Eric **sent a Christmas postcard to me**.
4형식: Eric **sent me a Christmas postcard**.

51 Sam은 우리를 위해 저녁을 만드는 중이다. (make)

3형식: Sam _____ _____ _____ _____ _____

4형식: Sam _____ _____ _____ _____

52 당신의 여권을 저에게 보여 주세요. (Please, show, passport)

3형식: _____ _____ _____ _____ _____ _____

4형식: _____ _____ _____ _____ _____

53 나는 엄마를 위해 새 지갑을 사야 해. (have to, buy, wallet)

3형식: _____ _____ _____ _____ _____ _____ _____

4형식: _____ _____ _____ _____ _____ _____ _____

3 & 4형식: 문장으로 영작 실력 다지기

정답 p. 119

54 Joe는 나에게 자주 많은 질문을 한다. (ask, many)

3형식: _____ _____ _____ _____ _____ _____

4형식: _____ _____ _____ _____ _____ _____

55 나는 어제 니콜에게 30달러를 빌려주었다. (lend, Nicole, $30)

3형식: _____ _____ _____ _____ _____ _____

4형식: _____ _____ _____ _____ _____ _____

56 나를 위해 빵 좀 사다 줄래? (will, get, some)

3형식: _____ _____ _____ _____ _____ _____ _____

4형식: _____ _____ _____ _____ _____ _____

57 유키 선생님은 학생들에게 일본어를 가르치신다. (Miss Yuki, Japanese)

3형식: _____ _____ _____ _____ _____ _____ _____

4형식: _____ _____ _____ _____ _____ _____

3 & 4형식 : 문장으로 영작 실력 다지기

정답 p. 119

58 (나의) 엄마는 매일 밤 나에게 이야기를 읽어 주신다. (stories, right)

3형식: _____ _____ _____ _____ _____ _____ _____

4형식: _____ _____ _____ _____ _____ _____ _____

59 파티마는 자주 그녀의 어머니께 꽃을 드린다. (Fatima, give)

3형식: _____ _____ _____ _____ _____ _____ _____

4형식: _____ _____ _____ _____ _____ _____ _____

60 그들은 그들의 부모님을 위해 집을 지을 것이다. (will, build)

3형식: _____ _____ _____ _____ _____ _____ _____

4형식: _____ _____ _____ _____ _____ _____ _____

5형식

[01-15] 알맞은 단어를 선택하시오. (2개 선택 가능)

01 He advised me _____ the job.

① not to take ② not take ③ not taking
④ not to be taken ⑤ not to taking

02 Can you help me _____ the kitchen next Saturday?

① to paint ② painting ③ painted
④ paint ⑤ paints

03 I told him _____ the volume down.

① put ② putting ③ to putting
④ to put ⑤ puts

04 My daughter wants me to let her _____ overnight at her friend's place.

① to stay ② staying ③ stayed
④ stay ⑤ stays

05 The supporters expect the manager _____ at least for one more season.

① to be stay ② staying ③ stay
④ to staying ⑤ to stay

06 I can order you _____ all the desks.

① to move ② moving ③ moved
④ move ⑤ moves

07 Her parents _____ her to stay out late on school nights.

① don't let ② don't allow ③ doesn't make
④ have ⑤ don't have

5형식

08 Claire didn't expect me _____ the exam.

① passed ② passing ③ to pass
④ passes ⑤ to passing

09 We need to get our neighbors _____ having loud parties every Saturday.

① stopping ② to stop ③ stop
④ stopped ⑤ to be stopped

10 The students asked the teacher _____ their test until the following week.

① will postpone ② postpone ③ postponed
④ to postpone ⑤ postponing

*postpone: 연기하다, 미루다

11 The teacher encouraged us _____ these math questions.

① figuring out ② to figure out ③ figure out
④ figured out ⑤ figures out

*figure out: 알아내다, (양·비용을) 계산하다

12 The doctor is only allowing people who are family members _____ the patient.

① to visit ② visiting ③ visits
④ visited ⑤ visit

13 My colleague asked _____ an email to the customer.

① me to sent ② my send ③ me send
④ me sending ⑤ me to send

*colleague 동료

14 My boss _____ me to take time off when my son was in the hospital.

① let ② made ③ allowed
④ help ⑤ persuades

15 A good teacher should motivate students _____ their best.

① to do ② do ③ does
④ doing ⑤ done

5형식

16 다음 문장의 빈칸에 들어갈 말로 적절한 것은?

Mr. Novak doesn't want us _____ in the playground.

① to play ② play ③ played ④ playing ⑤ plays

17 다음 문장의 빈칸에 들어갈 말로 적절한 것은?

They get me _____ new words.

① learn ② to learn ③ learns ④ learning ⑤ learned

18 다음 문장의 빈칸에 들어갈 말로 적절한 것은? (정답 2개)

We helped them _____ their houses.

① clean ② to clean ③ cleaning ④ cleaned ⑤ cleans

19 다음 문장의 빈칸에 들어갈 말로 적절한 것은?

The teacher told the children _____ down quietly.

① sat ② to sit ③ sit ④ sitting ⑤ sits

20 다음 문장의 빈칸에 들어갈 말로 적절하지 않은 것은?

Mrs. Smith _____ us do our assignment.

① let ② expected ③ made ④ helped ⑤ had

21 다음 문장의 빈칸에 들어갈 말로 적절하지 않은 것은?

I _____ him drive the car.

① let ② made ③ helped ④ had ⑤ allowed

22 다음 문장의 빈칸에 들어갈 말로 적절하지 않은 것을 모두 고르면?

He always _____ him to do that.

① lets ② has ③ allows ④ helps ⑤ makes

5형식

23 다음 우리말에 맞도록 알맞게 영작한 것은? (정답 2개)

> 샐리는 매일 밤 내가 숙제 하는 것을 도와 준다.

① Sally helps me do my homework every night.
② Sally helps me to do my homework every night.
③ Sally help me to do my homework every night.
④ Sally helps me doing my homework every night.
⑤ Sally helped me to do my homework every night.

24 다음 우리말에 맞도록 알맞게 영작한 것은?

> 그녀는 그에게 진실을 말하지 말라고 간청했다.

① She asked him to not tell the truth.
② She asked him not to tell the truth.
③ She didn't ask him not to tell the truth.
④ She didn't ask him to tell the truth.
⑤ She asked him not tell the truth.

25 다음 우리말에 맞도록 알맞게 영작한 것은?

> 새라는 내가 그 일에 지원하도록 설득했다.

① Sarah persuaded me apply for the job.
② Sarah persuaded I to apply for the job.
③ Sarah persuades me to apply for the job.
④ Sarah persuaded me to apply for the job.
⑤ Sarah persuaded me to be applied for the job.

26 다음 중 어법상 옳은 문장을 모두 고르시오.

① The injury caused him lose the game.
② My parents wouldn't allow me going to the party.
③ He watched Blake run down the stairs.
④ The teacher forced the kids to clean the classroom.
⑤ Mrs. Harrison doesn't want us to know the accident.

5형식

27 다음 중 어법상 옳은 문장을 모두 고르시오.

① They will get the report completed by tomorrow.

② I asked him to look at the picture.

③ Jenny could hear them arguing outside.

④ She heard Tom to go upstairs.

⑤ She made her own bread.

28 다음 중 어법상 틀린 문장은? (정답 2개)

① We listend to the rain falling.

② I told him to call the police.

③ David's mother let him to use her car.

④ We don't wish our names to appear in the newspaper.

⑤ He advised me not sell my house.

29 다음 중 어법상 틀린 문장을 모두 고르시오.

① He caused her to make a mistake.

② The commander forced the soldiers to march in the rain.

③ We invited them join us.

④ They helped their neighbor fix his car.

⑤ John got his son to wash the car.

⑥ We need someone to help us.

⑦ She persuaded him to have lunch with her.

*march: 행군하다

30 다음 괄호 (A), (B), (C), (D)에서 어법상 알맞은 말로 바르게 연결된 것은?

- I want him (A) [eat / to eat / eating] some pizza.
- They advised her (B) [go / to go / going] to university.
- He forced me (C) [sing / to sing / singing] a song.
- She got her daughter (D) [do / to do / doing] the dishes.

① (A) eat　　　(B) going　　(C) sing　　　(D) do
② (A) to eat　　(B) to go　　(C) singing　　(D) to do
③ (A) eating　　(B) going　　(C) singing　　(D) doing
④ (A) eat　　　(B) go　　　(C) sing　　　(D) do
⑤ (A) to eat　　(B) to go　　(C) to sing　　(D) to do

5형식 : 문장으로 영작 실력 다지기

정답 p. 121

[31-45] 괄호 안의 단어를 사용하여 빈칸을 완성하시오. (필요시 단어 변형)

31 그 농담은 그를 화나게 만들었다. (joke, make)

_____ _____ _____ _____ _____

32 루이스는 그 벽을 파란색으로 칠할 것이다. (paint)

_____ _____ _____ _____ _____
_____

33 헬렌은 우리에게 조용히 해 달라고 요청했다. (ask, quiet)

_____ _____ _____ _____ _____
_____

34 우리는 그 여자아이들이 춤추고 있는 것을 (일부만) 봤어. (see, dance)

_____ _____ _____ _____ _____

35 그녀는 매주 그녀의 옷을 세탁하도록 시킨다. (have, clothes, wash, week)

_____ _____ _____ _____ _____
_____ _____

5형식 : 문장으로 영작 실력 다지기

36 내가 나무 아래에서 자도록 해 줘. (let, under, the)

_____ _____ _____ _____ _____

_____

37 나는 그녀에게 시험 공부를 하라고 조언했다. (advise, for, exam)

_____ _____ _____ _____ _____

_____ _____ _____

38 우리는 그를 대통령으로 선출했다. (elect)

_____ _____ _____ _____

39 그녀는 옆방에서 아기가 우는 것을 들었다. (hear, a, cry, in, next)

_____ _____ _____ _____ _____

_____ _____ _____

40 그는 딸에게 방을 청소하게 했다. (get, clean, the)

_____ _____ _____ _____ _____

_____ _____ _____

5형식 : 문장으로 영작 실력 다지기

정답 p. 121

41 내가 너랑 해변에 같이 가길 원해? (want, go with, to)

D_____ y_____ _____ _____ _____
_____ _____ _____ _____ _____ _____
_____

42 케이트는 카페에서 만나자고 그녀의 친구에게 말했다. (Kate, tell, meet, at)

_____ _____ _____ _____ _____ _____
_____ her _____ _____ _____ _____

43 나는 내 남동생에게 내 여행 가방을 들게 했다. (have, carry, suitcase)

_____ _____ m_____ b_____ _____ _____
_____ _____

44 너 다음 토요일에 나 꽃 심는 것 좀 도와줄 수 있어? (Can, plant, next)

_____ _____ _____ _____ _____ _____
_____ _____ _____ _____

45 우리 부모님은 매일 아침 새들이 지저귀는 소리를 들으신다. (listen, birds, singing)

_____ _____ _____ _____ _____ _____
_____ _____ _____ _____

종합문제

정답 p. 121

[01-05] 문장의 형식을 쓰시오.

01 A) There is a pencil on the book. (   ) 형식   B) My hobby is collecting coins. (   ) 형식
      C) He grows many flowers in his garden. (   ) 형식   D) He sent his friend a postcard. (   ) 형식
      E) I went to the store. (   ) 형식

02 A) I saw Mary cross the street. (   ) 형식   B) I made her happy. (   ) 형식
      C) The rabbit hopped. (   ) 형식   D) Ellen wrote a letter to Mr. Green. (   ) 형식
      E) Two ducks were swimming. (   ) 형식

03 A) The fireworks exploded loudly. (   ) 형식   B) I bought her a gift. (   ) 형식
      C) My dad is a teacher. (   ) 형식   D) He had a great time yesterday. (   ) 형식
      E) The telephone rang loudly. (   ) 형식

04 A) There are three dogs in the house. (   ) 형식   B) She made her children clean their rooms. (   ) 형식
      C) Leaves turn brown in the fall. (   ) 형식   D) He passed the salt to his sister. (   ) 형식
      E) Please, let me borrow your pen. (   ) 형식

05 A) She baked her friends a delicious cake. (   ) 형식
      B) The coach had the team practice for hours. (   ) 형식
      C) The flowers look beautiful. (   ) 형식
      D) She gave a hug to her friend. (   ) 형식
      E) They named their puppy Sparky. (   ) 형식

[06-20] 괄호 안의 단어를 활용하여 문장을 완성하시오. (필요시 단어 변형)

06 벽에는 시계가 있다. (There, clock, wall)

_____

07 그 기차는 일찍 도착했다. (arrive, early)

_____

종합문제

08 일본 홋카이도는 겨울에 눈이 많이 온다. (snow, lot, in Hokkaido)

It _____ _____ _____ _____ _____ _____ _____ _____.

09 누군가가 호수에서 수영하고 있다. (Somebody, swim)

_____ _____ _____ _____ _____ _____ _____.

10 모든 사람은 많은 면에서 특별합니다. (Everyone, special, in)

_____ _____ _____ _____ w_____.

11 그 바람은 내 얼굴에 시원한 느낌이 들게 한다. (The, feel, on)

_____ wind _____ _____ _____ _____ _____.

12 Kate는 건강하고 행복해 보여. (well)

_____ _____ _____ _____ _____.

13 여기는 겨울에는 아주 일찍 어두워집니다. (get)

It _____ _____ _____ _____ _____ _____ _____.

14 아빠는 설거지를 하고 계셔. (wash, dishes)

_____ _____ _____ _____ _____.

종합문제

15 Ann은 일주일에 한번 테니스를 친다. (play, once)

_____ _____ _____ _____ _____ _____

16 너는 그녀에게 물을 조금 가져다 줄 수 있겠니? (Can, bring)

_____ _____ _____ _____ _____ _____ _____

17 우리는 Katie에게 장난감 집을 만들어 주고 싶습니다. (would like, build, playhouse)

_____ _____ _____ _____ _____ _____ _____

_____

18 이 책은 그녀를 유명하게 만들었다. (make, famous)

_____ _____ _____ _____ _____

19 나는 네가 영어를 배웠으면 좋겠어. (want, learn)

_____ _____ _____ _____ _____ _____

20 내가 그 편지를 좀 볼게. (have, look, at)

Let _____ _____ _____ _____ _____ _____

_____

꼭 알아야 하는 영문법

workbook

8품사·문장성분·5형식

8품사

문장성분과 5형식

꼭 알아야 하는 영문법
8품사 workbook

정답 p. 122

[01-08] 〈보기〉 단어의 알맞은 품사를 써 넣으시오. (총 29단어)

him	John	young	but	of	badly	speak	at
we	write	Austria	cold	useful	pig	because	great
sadness	death	here	oops	hey	always	you	or
about	them	slowly	sing	South America			

01 명사: _____

02 대명사: _____

03 동사: _____

04 형용사: _____

05 부사: _____

06 전치사: _____

07 접속사: _____

08 감탄사: _____

[09-13] 〈대명사+be 동사〉를 사용하여 빈칸을 완성하시오.

09 A) Sue is a student. ___She is___ from Canada.
B) Jim is a doctor. _____ kind to his patients.
C) I have one sister. _____ twelve years old.
D) My uncles are farmers. _____ very diligent.

*patient: 환자   *diligent: 부지런한

10 A) Lisa and I are in the same class. _____ good friends.
B) This book is interesting. _____ about ancient history.
C) There are some pies on the table. _____ for you.
D) I'm not from this town. _____ from another city.

*ancient: 고대의

11 A) Jane has a cat and a dog. _____ both very cute and friendly.
B) My parents work at a hospital. _____ doctors who help sick people.
C) Today is Monday. _____ the first day of the week.
D) You and your friend are happy. _____ smiling.

12 A) I know you. _____ Kate's sister.
B) I live in a house. _____ bigger than my old one.
C) I like your dogs. _____ cute.
D) I feel a little tired. _____ not going to the park today.

13 A) My friends and I are on the same team. _____ excited.
B) Emily is my cousin. _____ a great singer.
C) Tom is my brother. _____ good at soccer.
D) Ben and Lucy are in the library. _____ reading books.

[14-18] 〈대명사: 주격, 목적격, 소유 대명사〉를 사용하여 빈칸을 완성하시오.

14 A) Justin loves Kate. ____He____ loves ____her____ very much.

B) John has a new car. _____ is expensive.

C) I have three pictures on my bedroom. I like _____. _____ are wonderful.

D) I can't find my keys. Can you help _____ look for _____?

15 A) I think these keys are not _____. So, I left them on the table.

B) My sister and I have bikes. They are _____.

C) I know Mr. and Mrs. Smith. Do you know _____ too?

D) Rod has a car. _____ bought _____ last month.

16 A) I think I saw John drop this pen. I think it is _____.

B) Penguins don't live near the North Pole. _____ live near the South Pole.

C) My sister lives in Beijing, but _____ often comes to visit _____. _____ are close.

D) That jacket belongs to you. Is this blue one _____, too?

*the North Pole: 북극   *the South Pole: 남극   *close: 가까운   *belong to: 속해 있다

17 A) David wrote a letter, but _____ can't send _____ because she doesn't have a stamp.

B) We know those students. _____ are in the soccer club, and that ball is _____.

C) The white backpack is Emily's. It is _____.

D) A: Where are your friends?

B: I don't know. _____ are very late.

18 A) A: I can't find my pen. Can I use _____?

B: Sure.

B) A: Have you seen my children?

B: Yes, _____ are playing with their friends in the park.

C) Olivia didn't bring an umbrella, so I gave _____ _____.

D) This book is boring. I don't like _____.

[19-38] 다음 중 밑줄 친 부분에 품사가 다른 하나는?

19
① I like the <u>color</u> of your shirt.
② She picked a red <u>color</u> for her new car.
③ He <u>colored</u> the map to highlight different regions.
④ The room was painted in a bright <u>color</u>.
⑤ The crayons have many different <u>colors</u>.

*highlight: 강조 표시를 하다   *region: 지역

20
① She speaks <u>well</u>.
② The team worked <u>well</u> together on the project.
③ Did you sleep <u>well</u>?
④ The festival was very <u>well</u> organized.
⑤ Are you <u>well</u>?

*organized: 조직화된, 계획된

21
① We will have to <u>work</u> until midnight.
② His <u>work</u> permit expires next month.
③ She came home after finishing a hard day's <u>work</u>.
④ There is a lot of <u>work</u> to be done by tomorrow.
⑤ This <u>work</u> requires the cooperation of the team.

*expire: 만료되다   *require: 요구하다   *cooperation: 협동

22
① I take a 30-minute <u>break</u> during lunchtime.
② She needs a short <u>break</u> during her busy day.
③ We take a long <u>break</u> once a week.
④ He accidentally <u>broke</u> the window.
⑤ The trip was a great <u>break</u> from the routine.

*accidentally: 우연히

23
① I decided to <u>change</u> my hairstyle.
② He <u>changed</u> his mind and made different plans.
③ A small <u>change</u> can make a big difference.
④ The weather suddenly <u>changed</u>.
⑤ She <u>changed</u> her clothes and went to the party.

24
① The judge made a fair decision in the case.
② It is important to have a fair competition for everyone.
③ We visited the book fair last weekend.
④ She was praised for her fair treatment of all employees.
⑤ The teacher made sure to give every student a fair chance to participate.

*judge: 판사   *case: 소송   *participate: 참가하다, 참석하다

25
① She is pretty.
② The flowers are pretty.
③ The dress looks pretty on her.
④ The sunset is pretty tonight.
⑤ It's pretty cold today.

26
① We made an order for office supplies.
② We received our food order within 30 minutes.
③ Colin and Jake ordered pizza for dinner.
④ I placed an order for a book online.
⑤ It took time for the order to arrive.

*office supplies: 사무용품

27
① He is facing a big challenge.
② She had to face problems at work.
③ The team has to face a strong opponent.
④ Her face was filled with a happy expression.
⑤ The president faces the difficult task.

*opponent: 상대

28
① Birds fly south for the winter to find warmer climates.
② There was a fly buzzing around the kitchen.
③ They flew across the ocean to reach their destination.
④ He dreams of being a pilot, so he can fly airplanes around the world.
⑤ The kite flew high in the sky, carried by the strong wind.

*climate: 기후   *buzz: 윙윙거리다   *destination: 목적지

29
① The athlete ran fast to win the race.
② The news spread fast through social media.
③ Kids grow up fast these days.
④ I'm a fast learner.
⑤ How fast can you get the job done?

30
① He had a knife in his right hand.
② You have the right to remain silent.
③ She sits on the right side of the classroom.
④ She moved the book to the right shelf.
⑤ Take the next right turn.

31
① The company will train its employees on the new software next week.
② He trained hard to improve his basketball skills.
③ We took the train from Paris to London for our vacation.
④ We need to train the new puppy to sit and stay.
⑤ She trains with a personal trainer at the gym three times a week.

32
① The marathon race will start at 8 AM tomorrow.
② Stevens will not race in the final due to a knee injury.
③ She trained for months to compete in the bicycle race.
④ We organized a fun race for the kids at the park.
⑤ Over 80 cars will take part in the race.

*due to: ~때문에

33
① The present situation could get much worse.
② She received a beautiful present for her birthday.
③ He gave me a thoughtful present that made my day.
④ The children were excited to unwrap their Christmas presents.
⑤ I bought a small present for my friend to cheer her up.

*thoughtful : 사려 깊은

34
① He will run the marathon next month.
② I ran down the stairs as fast as I could.
③ She went for a morning run in the park.
④ The kids run around the playground every day.
⑤ She turned and ran away.

35
① This is the last book on the shelf.
② We need to last through the entire marathon without giving up.
③ She wore the same dress for the last three days.
④ The last train leaves at midnight.
⑤ I didn't read the last chapter of the book.

*entire: 전체의

36
① She booked a table at the restaurant for dinner.
② They booked tickets for the concert in advance.
③ I borrowed a book from the library.
④ Harry and Louise were disappointed because they didn't book a camping site.
⑤ I need to book a hotel room for next week.

*in advance: 미리, 사전에

37
① What does this word mean?
② I didn't mean to hurt you.
③ This symbol means peace.
④ Don't be so mean to her!
⑤ Now, I knew what they meant.

38
① Let's plant some flowers in the garden.
② They decided to plant a tree in the backyard.
③ We should plant these seeds before the rain comes.
④ This is a beautiful plant.
⑤ We've planted tomatoes and carrots in the garden.

[39-40] 다음 글에서 명사(13개)와 대명사(3개)를 모두 찾아 쓰시오. (소유격은 제외)

Justin Bieber is a famous singer with a lot of fans. His songs are loved by many people. The fans enjoy his music and performances. Justin often wears cool clothes and sunglasses. This makes him look stylish. At concerts, the audience sings along with him and cheers loudly.

39 명사: _____

40 대명사: _____

다음 글에서 본동사를 모두 찾아 쓰시오. (총 6개)

The Premier League is a well-known soccer league in England. It has many great teams like Manchester United, Liverpool, and Tottenham Hotspur. People all over the world watch the games. The matches are very exciting and the players are very skilled. Fans love to see their favorite teams win.

41 동사: _____

다음 글에서 형용사를 모두 찾아 쓰시오. (총 10개)

The Great Wall of China is a famous landmark that attracts many visitors. It was built a long time ago to protect China from invaders. Construction started more than 2,000 years ago and continued for many centuries. The Wall is very long, stretching over 13,000 miles. It is made of different materials like earth, wood, and stone. Today, the Great Wall is a popular place for tourists and a symbol of China's rich history.

=landmark: 주요 지형지물   *construction: 건설, 건축

42 형용사: Great, _____

다음 글에서 부사를 모두 찾아 쓰시오. (총 9개)

Today, I enjoyed a very tasty and special meal. Mom carefully cooked the rice, which was hot and soft, and it went perfectly with spicy kimchi and delicious side dishes. I happily ate crispy fish with fresh, crunchy lettuce. The fish was incredibly moist and flavorful, and the homemade sauce made it even more delightful. For dessert, I had sweet and juicy fruits that tasted really refreshing. It was a wonderful end to a definitely great meal.

43 부사: _____

_____

다음 글에서 전치사를 모두 찾아 쓰시오. (총 11개)

Elon Musk is renowned for his work in technology and space. He is the founder of SpaceX, where he builds rockets for traveling to space. Additionally, he started Tesla, which makes electric cars to promote a cleaner environment. While he works on these projects, he also thinks about new ideas for the future. Because he wants to help solve major problems, he often shares his plans with the public. Consequently, many people around the world are excited about his work and achievements.

*founder: 설립자   *promote: 촉진시키다   *achievement: 성취

44 전치사: _____

_____

다음 글에서 접속사를 모두 찾아 쓰시오. (총 9개)

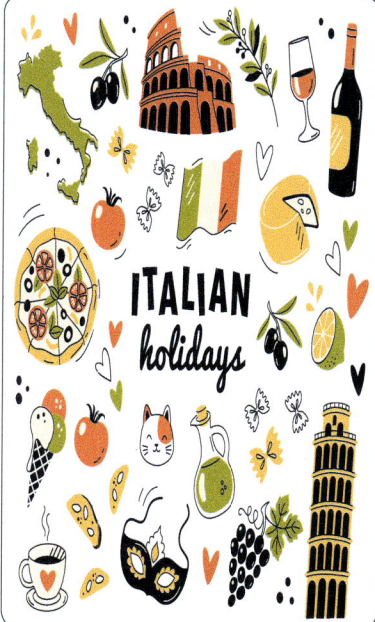

Last summer, we went on a wonderful trip to Italy, and it was an unforgettable experience. We visited the ancient Colosseum in Rome. We also had a chance to explore charming little towns in Tuscany when we traveled by car. We stayed in a lovely place with a beautiful view of the countryside. Each day, we tried new foods and experienced different cultures, so every moment felt exciting and new. Although the trip was filled with amazing sights and activities, we still wished we could have stayed longer. We ended our trip in Venice. For our final activity, we took a romantic gondola ride through the canals, and it was a perfect way to conclude our journey. The entire trip was amazing, but it went by quickly. I'm already looking forward to my next adventure.

*unforgettable: 잊을 수 없는   *canal: 수로

45 접속사: _____

다음 글에서 감탄사를 모두 찾아 쓰시오. (총 3개)

Wow, the weather is great today! The sky is clear, and the sunshine is warm. Oh, listen to the birds chirping. Ah, it's a waste to stay home on a day like this. The blooming flowers and playful puppies are so cute. It's a truly happy day!

*chirp: 짹짹거리다

46 감탄사: _____

[47-48] 다음 밑줄 친 단어의 품사를 쓰시오.

(A) Paris is a beautiful city. The Eiffel Tower (B) stands tall in the center of the city. (C) Many (D) tourists visit it each year. The (E) lively streets are filled (F) with cafes and shops. In the evening, the city (G) shines (H) brightly. People enjoy (I) walking (J) along the Seine River. Paris is known for its delicious food (K) and charming (L) architecture.

47 A) _____ B) _____ C) _____

D) _____ E) _____ F) _____

48 G) _____ H) _____ I) _____

J) _____ K) _____ L) _____

[49-52] 다음 밑줄 친 단어의 품사와 의미를 쓰시오.

The Earth is a (A) diverse planet. (B) It has many beautiful landscapes, including mountains and oceans. People live in different regions (C) around the globe. The weather (D) varies (E) greatly (F) from one (G) place to another. Some areas are very hot (H) while others are (I) cold. The Earth also has a (J) variety of (K) plants and animals. The planet (L) provides resources for all living things.

49 A) diverse   품사: _____   의미: _____

B) It   품사: _____   의미: _____

C) around   품사: _____   의미: _____

50 D) varies   품사: _____   의미: _____

E) greatly   품사: _____   의미: _____

F) from   품사: _____   의미: _____

정답 p. 125 **실전문제**

51 G) place   품사: _____   의미: _____

     H) while   품사: _____   의미: _____

     I) cold   품사: _____   의미: _____

52 J) variety   품사: _____   의미: _____

     K) plants   품사: _____   의미: _____

     L) provides   품사: _____   의미: _____

[53-56] 다음 밑줄 친 단어의 품사와 의미를 쓰시오.

(A) K-pop is a **(B)** popular music **(C)** genre from South Korea. It **(D)** mixes different music styles and **(E)** features **(F)** energetic performances. Many K-pop groups, like BTS and BLACKPINK, are famous around the world. Fans enjoy their exciting dance **(G)** moves and catchy songs. K-pop artists **(H)** work hard to create **(I)** unique music videos. The **(J)** influence of K-pop **(K)** is growing and bringing new trends to the **(L)** global music scene.

53 A) K-pop   품사: _____   의미: _____

     B) popular   품사: _____   의미: _____

     C) genre   품사: _____   의미: _____

54 D) mixes   품사: _____   의미: _____

     E) features   품사: _____   의미: _____

     F) energetic   품사: _____   의미: _____

55 G) moves   품사: _____   의미: _____

     H) work   품사: _____   의미: _____

     I) unique   품사: _____   의미: _____

56 J) influence   품사: _____   의미: _____

     K) is growing   품사: _____   의미: _____

     L) global   품사: _____   의미: _____

[57-60] 어법상 틀린 부분을 찾아 고치시오.

〈보기〉 You and your brothers often play video games together. We enjoy spending time together.　　**We** → **You**

57 A) Balancing work and family life can be a difficulty task for many people.　　_____ → _____

B) Their success campaign led to an increase in sales.　　_____ → _____

C) He stressed the importance points during the meeting.　　_____ → _____

58 A) Emma decided to move into a new house to start a new living.　　_____ → _____

B) Please put your sign here.　　_____ → _____

C) Cathy and her sisters are very talented artists. We create beautiful paintings.　　_____ → _____

59 A) George and me visited the Grand Canyon last summer.　　_____ → _____

B) Be on time! It means "Don't late."　　_____ → _____

C) I don't understand. Can you speak more clear?　　_____ → _____

60 A) We are talking about Janice and she.　　_____ → _____

B) Sarah borrowed the books from the library. It was very informative.　　_____ → _____

C) Sydney is famous for it's beaches.　　_____ → _____

*informative : 유용한 정보를 주는, 유익한

[61-62] 다음 글을 읽고, 물음에 답하시오.

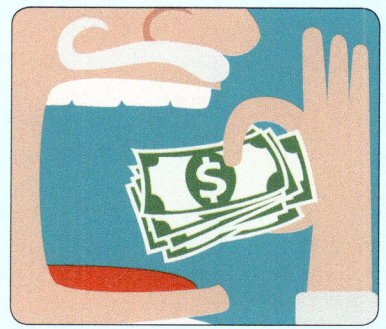

In a small village, there lived a man named, John, who was very **(A)** mean with his money. He never shared anything and always kept to himself. One day, his grandson, Michael, came home with a school assignment. He had to explain the meaning of the word "mean."

John explained, "The word 'mean' can have two meanings. It can describe someone who is not generous, **like** me sometimes. It can also **(B)** mean 'to signify' or 'to indicate something.'"

Michael thanked his grandfather and went to school the next day. During his presentation, he said, "My grandfather is sometimes **(C)** mean with his money, which **(D)** means he doesn't like to share. But the word 'mean' can also **(E)** mean 'to signify.'"

His classmates understood the two different meanings easily, and John felt happy that his explanation helped Michael with his assignment.

*assignment: 과제

61 다음 중 〈보기〉 mean의 의미와 같은 뜻으로 쓰인 것을 모두 고르시오.

〈보기〉 In the novel *A Christmas Carol*, Scrooge is known for being **mean** and miserly, particularly when it comes to money.

① (A)　　② (B)　　③ (C)　　④ (D)　　⑤ (E)

62 윗글의 like와 같은 의미로 쓰인 것을 모두 고르시오.

① How do you like living in London?
② I don't like the way he shouts at the children.
③ This sweater is soft, like the one I have at home.
④ Her voice sounds like a singer's.
⑤ He's never liked talking about people behind their backs.
⑥ The cat is friendly, like my other pets.
⑦ The book is interesting, like the last one I read.
⑧ One of the things I like about John is his sense of humor.

[63-64] 다음 글을 읽고, 물음에 답하시오.

The **(A)** work of Pablo Picasso is revolutionary. He changed the art world with his innovative techniques and unique perspectives. Picasso helped create cubism, a style that broke objects into abstract shapes. This new way of seeing things influenced many artists and changed how people think about art. His **(B)** bold use of color and form inspired others to be creative and try new things. Picasso's legacy shows how powerful and lasting innovation can be in the world of art.

*revolutionary: 혁명적인   *perspective: 원근법   *cubism: 입체파   *object: 물체
*abstract: 추상적인   *inspire: 영감을 주다   *legacy: 유산   *lasting: 지속적인

63 윗글의 (A) work의 의미와 같은 뜻으로 쓰인 것을 모두 고르시오.

① The gallery exhibited the work of several contemporary artists.
② Young people come to town looking for work.
③ His latest work is a masterpiece.
④ They admired the detailed work of the craftsman.
⑤ We work together to complete this project.
⑥ There isn't a lot of work at this time of the year.
⑦ This novel is considered one of his greatest works.
⑧ We both work for the same company.

*contemporary: 동시대의, 현대의   *admire: 감탄하다

64 윗글의 (B) bold의 의미와 같은 뜻으로 쓰인 것을 모두 고르시오.

① All the titles are in bold type to make them easier to read.
② His bold choice to speak up in the meeting impressed everyone.
③ She made a bold move by changing her career path completely.
④ His bold idea to travel alone across the country was exciting.
⑤ The chef's bold decision to try new ingredients made the dish unique.
⑥ The heading was in bold text to make it stand out.
⑦ The important points were written in bold to highlight them.

*stand out: 눈에 띄다

꼭 알아야 하는 영문법
문장성분과 5형식 workbook

1-5형식

문장형식	문장 구조		동사의 종류
1형식	주어+동사	S+V	완전 자동사
2형식	주어+동사+보어	S+V+C	불완전 자동사
3형식	주어+동사+목적어	S+V+O	완전 타동사
4형식	주어+동사+간접목적어-직접목적어	S+V+IO+DO	수여동사
5형식	주어+동사+목적어+목적격보어	S+V+O+OC	불완전 타동사

자동사 vs. 타동사

▶ **자동사**

run, sit 처럼 목적어를 수반하지 않는 동사들을 '자동사'라고 한다. 자동사를 수식하는 부사(구)나 전치사구는 올 수 있다.

- **I run**. 나는 달린다.
  주어 자동사

- Please, **sit down**. 앉아주세요.
  자동사 부사

- William **smokes too much**. 윌리엄은 담배를 많이 핀다.
  자동사 부사구

- **He works from Monday to Friday**. 그는 월요일부터 금요일까지 일한다.
  주어 자동사 전치사구

▶ **타동사**

like, surprise 처럼 목적어를 필요로 하는 동사를 '타동사'라고 한다.

- I **like Jack**. 나는 잭을 좋아한다.
  타동사 목적어

- The news **surprised me**. 그 소식은 나를 놀라게 했다.
  타동사 목적어

실전문제

[01-03] 다음 문장에 주어에는 S를, 동사에는 V를 쓰고 밑줄을 그으시오.

> 〈보기〉 <u>**I go**</u> to school at 8:30.
>   S V

01 A) William eats too much.   B) The phone rang repeatedly.

C) A lot of people went there.

02 A) Charlie goes to school every day.   B) Your essay reads well.

C) The train arrived early this morning.

03 A) The cat sleeps on the couch.   B) They swim in the lake.

C) The dog barks at strangers.

[04-06] 다음 문장에 주어에는 S를, 동사에는 V를, 보어에는 C를 쓰고 밑줄을 그으시오.

> 〈보기〉 <u>**I feel good**</u> today.
>   S   V   C

04 A) Frank is an architect.   B) Alice looked cute yesterday.

C) The soup tastes horrible.

*architect: 건축가

05 A) The sky appeared clear today.   B) The room seemed cozy last night.

C) The cookies baking in the oven smell delicious.

*cozy: 아늑한

06 A) The water felt cold this morning.   B) The music sounded amazing at the concert.

C) The child looked excited on his birthday.

[07-09] 다음 문장에 주어에는 S를, 동사에는 V를, 목적어에는 O를 쓰고 밑줄을 그으시오.

〈보기〉 <u>Eric</u> <u>met</u> <u>Ann</u> yesterday
       S   V   O

07 A) Betty parked the car in the car park.　　B) We took her to the station.

C) We enjoyed ourselves at the party.

08 A) I want to sleep now.　　B) Kate enjoys playing tennis.

C) Martin introduced his guests to us.

09 A) Gerald explained the situation to me.　　B) Don't say it to him.

C) Would you describe it for me, please?

[10-12] 다음 문장에 간접목적어에는 IO를, 직접목적어에는 DO를 쓰고 밑줄을 그으시오.

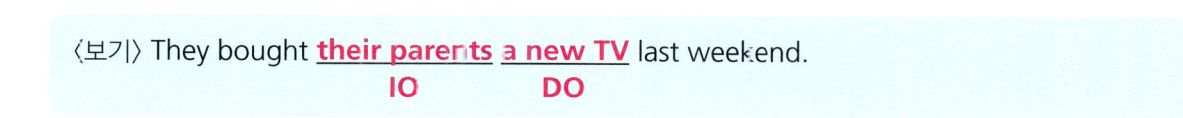

〈보기〉 They bought <u>their parents</u> <u>a new TV</u> last weekend.
                   IO   DO

10 A) We gave Sam a good watch.　　B) I sent Mike a parcel last week.

C) They offered her a promotion at work.

*parcel: 소포　*promotion: 승진

11 A) I brought my friend a souvenir from the trip.　　B) He showed us his new painting.

C) The teacher gives the students extra homework almost every day.

*souvenir: 기념품

12 A) She baked her neighbor a cake for her birthday.　　B) He lent his brother some money.

C) We served our guests a delicious meal for the celebration.

[13-15] 다음 문장에 주어에는 S를, 동사에는 V를, 목적어에는 O를, 목적격 보어에는 OC를 쓰고 밑줄을 그으시오.

> 〈보기〉 I painted the wall green.
>   S   V   O   OC

13 A) Loud music drives me crazy.　　B) They called him foolish.

C) We appointed her chairperson.

14 A) Keep it short, please.　　B) His jokes made us laugh all night.

C) The news made her happy this morning.

15 A) They elected him president.　　B) The movie left us speechless with its twist ending.

C) Sarah let her son decide for himself.

*speechless: (특히 너무 화가 나거나 놀라서) 말을 못 하는　　*twist ending: 반전

[16-20] 다음 문장의 형식을 고르시오.

16 A) We ate a lot this afternoon. (1형식, 2형식, 3형식)

B) There are many people at the park. (1형식, 2형식, 3형식)

C) You look smart today. (1형식, 2형식, 3형식)

D) I am writing a grammar book. (1형식, 2형식, 3형식)

17 A) I sometimes stay up until midnight. (1형식, 2형식, 3형식)

B) The soup tastes delicious. (1형식, 2형식, 3형식)

C) She reads a book every night. (1형식, 2형식, 3형식)

D) The sun rises early. (1형식, 2형식, 3형식)

18 A) The children laughed loudly. (1형식, 2형식, 3형식)

B) He is fixing his car at the moment. (1형식, 2형식, 3형식)

C) Birds fly south for the winter. (1형식, 2형식, 3형식)

D) The flowers smell absolutely wonderful. (1형식, 2형식, 3형식)

19 A) We like to listen to music. (1형식, 2형식, 3형식)

B) This chair feels extremely comfortable. (1형식, 2형식, 3형식)

C) It rained heavily yesterday. (1형식, 2형식, 3형식)

D) They have built a new house. (1형식, 2형식, 3형식)

20 A) He seems tired today. (1형식, 2형식, 3형식)

B) The sky turned gray. (1형식, 2형식, 3형식)

C) She painted a beautiful picture. (1형식, 2형식, 3형식)

D) Luna often laughs. (1형식, 2형식, 3형식)

[21-25] 다음 문장의 형식을 고르시오.

21 A) My mother cooked Mary chicken soup. (3형식, 4형식, 5형식)

B) I saw Henry walking the dog in the park. (3형식, 4형식, 5형식)

C) I am going to sell my car. (3형식, 4형식, 5형식)

D) Do you ever eat meat? (3형식, 4형식, 5형식)

22 A) My sister wears glasses. (3형식, 4형식, 5형식)

B) My brother bought Lisa a new book. (3형식, 4형식, 5형식)

C) She heard Peter singing loudly in the shower. (3형식, 4형식, 5형식)

D) We will visit our grandparents next weekend. (3형식, 4형식, 5형식)

23 A) Does she often watch movies on weekends? (3형식, 4형식, 5형식)

B) She taught her students French vocabulary every day. (3형식, 4형식, 5형식)

C) They threw their friend a surprise birthday party last weekend. (3형식, 4형식, 5형식)

D) I don't think that I like her. (3형식, 4형식, 5형식)

24 A) She painted her bedroom blue. (3형식, 4형식, 5형식)

B) We named our new puppy Max. (3형식, 4형식, 5형식)

C) They appointed her the new manager. (3형식, 4형식, 5형식)

D) Bill said that he was happy. (3형식, 4형식, 5형식)

25 A) She told me to get out. (3형식, 4형식, 5형식)

B) Stop complaining about your problems. (3형식, 4형식, 5형식)

C) Please, let him go. (3형식, 4형식, 5형식)

D) We had our car fixed yesterday. (3형식, 4형식, 5형식)

종합문제

[26-35] 다음 문장의 형식을 쓰시오.

26 A) There is a pencil on the desk. _____
B) One of my hobbies is collecting key rings. _____
C) I didn't expect them to be here. _____
D) He cultivates many roses in his garden. _____
E) Louise warned me not to play with matches. _____

*cultivate: 경작하다 *match: 성냥

27 A) I saw Mary crossing the road. _____
B) The rabbit hopped playfully. _____
C) Ellen sent Mr. Smith a letter. _____
D) Two ducks were gracefully swimming. _____
E) I made her extremely happy. _____

*gracefully: 우아하게

28 A) The fireworks exploded loudly over the city. _____
B) Billy has written a eight-page letter to Chris. _____
C) At school, our teacher made us work hard. _____
D) The telephone suddenly rang loudly. _____
E) He had a fantastic time yesterday. _____

*explode: 폭발하다

29 A) There are three playful dogs in the yard. _____
B) She made her children tidy their rooms. _____
C) Leaves gradually turn golden in the fall. _____
D) He passed the pepper to his sister. _____
E) Could you please lend me your calculator for a moment? _____

playful: 장난기 많은 *gradually: 점차적으로 *calculator: 계산기

30 A) She baked a delicious pie for her friends. _____
B) The coach had the team practice diligently for hours. _____
C) The colorful flowers are beautiful in the garden. _____
D) She gave her friend a warm hug. _____
E) Ava found the book boring. _____

*diligently: 부지런히

31
A) An opportunity like this comes once in a lifetime. _____
B) That cute girl is drinking milk now. _____
C) The police caught the robbers yesterday. _____
D) Can you pass Mr. Anderson this newspaper? _____
E) Your hands are very cold. _____

*once in a lifetime: 평생 단 한 번뿐인

32
A) The tall man has just painted the walls. _____
B) The students have solved some mathematics problems. _____
C) You mustn't smoke too much. _____
D) Are you thirsty? _____
E) Paul told them not to wait for him. _____

33
A) The cook has made some chocolate cakes. _____
B) Smoking is bad for you. _____
C) Our train leaves at 9:10. _____
D) I'm working today. _____
E) Take Jack these boxes. _____

34
A) I've made coffee for everybody. _____
B) I have my hair cut every month. _____
C) What happened to Emily? _____
D) He wants me to cook dinner. _____
E) He ate quickly. _____

35
A) See me before you go. _____
B) Everest is the highest mountain in the world. _____
C) Jo drives more carefully than Sam. _____
D) He knew that he made a big mistake. _____
E) John asked Peter to close the door. _____

정답 pp. 129-130 **실전문제**

[36-50] 다음 문장의 형식을 쓰고, 각 성분을 분석한 내용을 작성하시오.

〈보기〉 My mother takes care of my little brother every day.　　　　**3** 형식
　　　　주어: **My mother**　　　　동사구: **takes care of**
　　　　목적어: **my little brother**　　　　수식어 (부사구): **every day**

36 She sings beautifully.　　　　_____형식

주어: _____　　　동사: _____

수식어: _____

37 She gave me a book that she likes.　　　　_____형식

38 The sun rises in the east every morning.　　　　_____형식

39 This exercise is extremely exhausting.　　　　_____형식

40 I have seen her dancing.　　　　_____형식

41 I am interested in sports.　　　　_____형식

42 Before I went out, I called John. _____형식

43 Hot weather makes me feel tired. _____형식

44 Her mother suggested that she should go and see the doctor. _____형식

45 We decided not to play baseball because of the weather. _____형식

46 Show me how to do it. _____형식

47 We are leaving tomorrow. _____형식

48 I wonder if you could help me. _____형식

49 We went out in spite of the rain. _____형식

50 Since it was a national holiday, all the post offices were closed. _____형식

꼭 알아야 하는 영문법

정답 및 해설집

8품사·문장성분·5형식

8품사

문장성분과 5형식

workbook

8품사

문장성분과 5형식

꼭 알아야 하는 영문법
8품사

정답 및 해설집

01 A) 부사　　B) 대명사　　C) 감탄사　　D) 접속사　　E) 전치사

02 A) 형용사　　B) 전치사　　C) 명사　　D) 대명사

03 A) 감탄사　　B) 동사　　C) 부사　　D) 접속사

04 ②　　**05** ③　　**06** ①　　**07** ③　　**08** ②

09 ②　　**10** ⑤　　**11** ④　　**12** ③　　**13** ③

14 명사: dog, car, woman, boy, bed

15 대명사: she, this, it

16 동사: have, eat

17 형용사: bad, new, big

18 부사: slowly, really, quickly

19 전치사: on, for, of

20 접속사: and, but

21 감탄사: wow, oh

22 ① 대명사　② 동사　③ 명사　④ 접속사　⑤ 명사

23 ① 명사　② 접속사　③ 대명사　④ 동사　⑤ 명사

24 ① 명사　② 동사　③ 형용사

25 <u>He</u> is <u>very</u> <u>cold</u>.
　　대명사　　부사　형용사

26 <u>They</u> are <u>nice</u>.
　　대명사　　형용사

27 <u>We</u> <u>like</u> <u>apples</u>.
　　대명사 동사　명사

28 <u>Wow</u>! Your girlfriend is <u>really</u> <u>beautiful</u>.
　　감탄사　　　　　　　　　　부사　　형용사

29 <u>I</u> <u>live</u> <u>in</u> <u>Tokyo</u> <u>but</u> <u>he</u> <u>lives</u> <u>in</u> <u>Sydney</u>.
　　대명사 동사 전치사 명사 접속사 대명사 동사 전치사 명사

30 ① 명사(시계) ② 동사(시청하다, 보다) ③ 명사(상점) ④ 동사(장을 보다)

31 ① 형용사(느린) ② 동사(속도를 늦추다) ③ 동사(색을 칠하다) ④ 명사(색깔)

32 ① 명사(반지) ② 동사(종이나 벨을 울리다) ③ 동사(일하다) ④ 명사(일)

33 ① 동사(물을 주다) ② 명사(물) ③ 동사(지속되다) ④ 형용사(지난)

34 ③: ③번의 watch는 동사로서 '시청하다,' '보다'의 의미이지만, 나머지는 명사로 '시계'의 의미이다.

정답 및 해설집

35 ④: ④번의 fast는 형용사로서 '빠른'의 의미이지만, 나머지는 부사로 '빠르게'의 의미이다.

36 ①: ①번의 play는 명사로서 '연극'의 의미이지만, 나머지는 동사로 쓰였다.
②번과 ⑤번은 '연주하다', ③번은 '~놀이하다', ④번은 '게임하다'라는 의미이다.

37 ①: ①번의 early는 부사로서 '이르게'의 의미이지만, 나머지는 형용사로 '이른'의 의미이다.

38 A) She   B) He   C) They   D) It   E) We

39 A) they   B) she   C) it   D) he   E) they

40 A) they   B) she   C) they   D) it   E) we

41 A) they   B) it   C) they   D) it   E) you

42 A) it   B) you   C) we   D) they   E) he

43 A) **Jason** likes the **movie** about **France**.　B) The **musicians** play great **songs**.
C) **Boys** and **girls** have the same **chances**.　D) A lot of **people** speak **English**.

44 A) **You** and John are the most important players.　B) Mr. Smith gave **us** the chocolate.
C) **They** sent **it** as a birthday gift.　D) Jack and **I** like eating **them**.

45 A) They **go** to West Point and **watch** the parade.　B) Just **do** it.
C) It **is** a nice place. Many people **go** there on vacation.　D) She **cried** loudly, and both of us **heard** her.

46 A) You look **great** today.
B) My brother lives in a **new** house.
C) It is a **large round** table.
D) There are **many beautiful yellow** flowers in the garden.

47 A) Watch **very closely**.　B) My team played **badly**.
C) Go **slowly**. Look **carefully**. Walk **there**.　D) Ah! The sun is **so** warm.

48 A) Lucy **and** Ed left the door open.
B) He is going to school, **but** I am going to work.
C) He studied hard, **so** he passed the exam.
D) You can have ham, cheese, **or** tuna.

49 A) The knife is **on** the table.
B) I will see you **in** the morning.
C) Columbus made his first trip **from** Europe **to** America.
D) When they were **in** China, they spent a few days **in** Beijing.

50 A) **Oops**, I made a mistake again.　B) **Hurray**! We won the match.
C) **Wow**! Look at that!　D) **Oh** no, I forgot to turn off the stove!

정답 및 해설집

51 late, brave, noisy, smart, young, easy

52 there, hardly, carefully, angrily

53 in, for, about, of, under

54 sick: sick는 형용사로 '아픈'의 의미이다. 나머지 명사

55 really: really는 부사로 '정말'의 의미이다. 나머지 형용사

56 and: and는 접속사로 '그리고'의 의미이다. 나머지 전치사

57 strong: strong은 형용사로 '강한'의 의미이다. 나머지 동사

58 true: true은 형용사로 '사실은'의 의미이다. 나머지 동사

59 certain: certain는 형용사로 '확실한' 또는 '틀림없는'의 의미이다. 나머지 부사

60 ②: ②번의 run은 동사로서 '뛰다'의 의미이지만, happy는 형용사로 '행복한'의 의미이다.

61 ③: ③번의 finish는 동사로서 '끝내다'의 의미이지만, late은 형용사로 '늦은', 부사로 '늦게'의 의미이다.

62 ④: ④번의 handsome은 형용사로서 '잘생긴'의 의미이지만, beauty는 명사로 '아름다움''의 의미이다.

63 ③: ③번의 Jason은 이름을 나타내는 명사이지만, he는 대명사로서 '그'의 의미이다.

64 ①: ①번의 you는 대명사로서 '너'의 의미이지만, Louise는 이름을 나타내는 명사이다.

65 ①: ①번의 about은 전치사로서 '~대한'의 의미이지만, but은 접속사로서 '그러나'의 의미이다.

혼동하기 쉬운 품사: 형용사와 부사

01 colorful: colorful은 형용사로 '다채로운'의 의미이다. 나머지 부사

02 lovely: lovely는 명사에 -ly가 붙은 형용사로 '사랑스러운'의 의미이다. 나머지 부사

03 seriously: seriously는 부사로 ' 심각하게' 또는 '진심으로'의 의미이다. 나머지 형용사

04 costly   boring   exciting   sick   cheap   quick

05 yesterday   soon   softly   greatly   heavily   terribly
*monthly는 명사에 -ly가 붙은 형용사로 '매달의'의 의미이다.

06 A) small, red   B) old, wooden   **07** A) interesting   B) long, beautiful

08 A) very, well   B) late   **09** A) clearly   B) always, early

10 A) beautifully   B) extremely   C) loudly   D) completely

정답 및 해설집

11 A) sweet B) late C) nice D) great

12 A) carefully B) quickly C) happily D) sad

13 A) surprisingly B) quietly C) beautifully D) correct

14 A) good B) really C) terribly D) slowly

15 A) 형용사 B) 부사 C) 부사 D) 부사

16 A) 부사, 형용사 B) 형용사, 형용사 C) 형용사 D) 형용사, 형용사

17 A) 형용사 B) 부사 C) 부사 D) 형용사

18 A) 형용사, 부사 B) 형용사 C) 형용사 D) 형용사

19 A) 부사, 형용사 B) 형용사 C) 형용사 D) 부사, 형용사

20 A) bad B) bad C) badly D) badly

21 A) hard B) hard C) hardly D) hardly

22 A) highly B) high C) high D) highly

23 A) late B) lately C) late D) lately

24 A) quickly B) quick C) quickly D) quick

25 ⑤: ⑤번은 동사를 꾸며주는 부사로 사용되었지만, 나머지는 형용사로 사용되었다.

26 ④: ④번은 동사를 꾸며주는 부사로 사용되었지만, 나머지는 형용사로 사용되었다.

27 ④: ④번은 주어를 보충 설명하는 형용사로 사용되었지만, 나머지는 동사를 꾸며주는 부사로 사용되었다.

28 ①: ①번은 동사를 꾸며주는 부사로 사용되었지만, 나머지는 형용사로 사용되었다.

29 ③: ③번은 동사를 꾸며주는 부사로 사용되었지만, 나머지는 형용사로 사용되었다.

30 ②: ②번은 명사를 꾸며주는 형용사로 사용되었지만, 나머지는 부사로 사용되었다.

31 ⑤: ⑤번은 동사를 꾸며주는 부사로 사용되었지만, 나머지는 형용사로 사용되었다.

32 ①: ①번은 형용사를 꾸며주는 부사로 사용되었지만, 나머지는 형용사로 사용되었다.

33 ②: ②번은 주어를 보충 설명하는 형용사로 사용되었지만, 나머지는 부사로 사용되었다.

34 A) well B) good C) good D) well

35 A) good B) well C) good D) well

36 A) quick, quickly B) careless, carelessly
C) nice, nicely D) badly, bad

정답 및 해설집

37 A) easily, easy   B) good, well
     C) beautiful, beautiful   D) slowly, dangerous

38 ④: 다음 문장은 아래와 같이 바꿔야 올바른 문장이 된다.
① I make a lot of money. I work very hard~~ly~~.
② Kate didn't sleep **well** last night.
③ She spoke soft**ly** to the children.
⑤ We must make decisions quick**ly**.

39 ②: 다음 문장은 아래와 같이 바꿔야 올바른 문장이 된다.
① Don't feel bad~~ly~~ about what happened last night.
③ They were **happily** married for 20 years.
④ He doesn't speak loud**ly**.
⑤ Your garden looks beautiful~~ly~~.

40 ②, ④, ⑥: 다음 문장은 아래와 같이 바꿔야 올바른 문장이 된다.
① I was late for work because the bus arrived late~~ly~~.
③ He had to stay late~~ly~~ at work to finish the report.
⑤ The chef prepared the meal perfect**ly**.
⑦ The flowers in the garden smell sweet~~ly~~.

41 ⑤: 다음 문장은 아래와 같이 바꿔야 올바른 문장이 된다.
⑤ She feels bad~~ly~~ about the mistake.

42 ①: 다음 문장은 아래와 같이 바꿔야 올바른 문장이 된다.
① He is a very **good** student.

43 A) good → well   B) angry → angrily   C) careful → carefully

44 A) happy → happily   B) hardly → hard   C) bad → badly

45 A) sudden → suddenly   B) quick → quickly   C) good → well

46 young, blue, wide, warm, quiet

47 little, small, green, sunny, gentle, fresh, perfect

48 beautifully, always, early, softly, happily

49 regularly, fast, high, carefully, fairly, happily

50 형용사: Last, beautiful, warm, sunny, old, many, interesting
부사: slowly, clearly

꼭 알아야 하는 영문법
문장성분과 5형식

정답 및 해설집

연습문제

01
A) <u>I</u> <u>work</u>.
   S   V

B) <u>I</u> <u>walk</u> <u>slowly</u>.
   S   V   M

C) <u>Jack</u> <u>is</u> <u>nice</u>.
   S   V   C

D) <u>Children</u> <u>like</u> <u>toys</u>.
    S   V   O

02
A) <u>My uncle</u> <u>is</u> <u>a farmer</u>.
    S   V   C

B) <u>I</u> <u>met</u> <u>Sally</u> <u>yesterday</u>.
   S V   O   M

C) <u>She</u> <u>is</u> very <u>kind</u>.
   S   V   C

D) <u>I</u> <u>like</u> <u>him</u>.
   S V   O

03
A) <u>We</u> often <u>play</u> <u>tennis and basketball</u>.
   S   V   O

B) <u>Sam</u> <u>read</u> many <u>books</u> <u>last year</u>.
   S   V   O   M

C) <u>The pasta</u> <u>looks</u> <u>delicious</u>.
    S   V   C

D) <u>The cat</u> <u>was</u> <u>black</u>.
    S   V   C

04
A) <u>I</u> <u>agree</u> <u>with you</u>.
   S V   M

B) <u>The cat</u> <u>is sleeping</u> <u>under the desk</u>.
    S   V   M

C) Don't <u>sit</u> <u>on the floor</u>.
      V   M

D) <u>We</u> <u>were</u> <u>late</u> <u>because of the heavy snow</u>.
   S   V   C   M

05
A) <u>I</u> <u>play</u> <u>tennis</u> <u>on Sundays</u>.
   S V   O   M

B) <u>The dog</u> <u>feels</u> <u>soft</u> and <u>warm</u>.
    S   V   C   C

C) <u>You</u> <u>look</u> <u>great</u> <u>today</u>.
   S   V   C   M

D) <u>They</u> <u>are washing</u> <u>their car</u>.
    S   V   O

06
A) <u>My hobby</u> <u>is</u> <u>running</u>.
    S   V   C

B) <u>Jack</u> <u>is</u> <u>good</u> <u>at painting ceilings</u>.
   S V C   M

C) <u>Robin</u> <u>brushes</u> <u>his teeth</u> <u>twice a day</u>.
    S   V   O   M

D) <u>Ava</u> doesn't <u>work</u> <u>in the morning</u>.
   S   V   M

07
A) <u>Henry</u> <u>lost</u> <u>his wallet</u> <u>yesterday</u>.
    S   V   O   M

B) <u>Isabella</u> <u>bought</u> <u>ice cream</u> <u>for us</u>.
    S   V   O   M

C) <u>My suit</u> <u>looks</u> <u>perfect</u>.
   S   V   C

D) <u>Always</u> <u>keep</u> <u>calm</u>.
   M   V   C

08 A) This novel is really interesting.
　　　　　　S　　V　M　　　C

　　　B) He began working at 8:00.
　　　　　S　V　　O　　　M

　　　C) Oliver reads a lot.
　　　　　S　　V　　M

　　　D) Today, I will cook dinner.
　　　　　　M　　S　　V　　O

09 A) Derek is a good writer.
　　　　　　S　　V　　　　C

　　　B) The train was late because of the accident.
　　　　　　S　　　V　　C　　　　　M

　　　C) Kevin looked nervous before his performance.
　　　　　S　　V　　　C　　　　M

　　　D) I will call a taxi for you.
　　　　　S　　V　　O　　M

10 A) Listen carefully!
　　　　　　V　　M

　　　B) This bus doesn't go to London.
　　　　　　S　　　V　　　M

　　　C) My brother writes with his left hand.
　　　　　　S　　　V　　　　M

　　　D) She only eats fish.
　　　　　S　　M　V　　O

● 1형식

01 A) The sun rises in the east.
　　　　　　S　　V

　　　B) They talked too loudly in the library.
　　　　　　S　　V

　　　C) I'm happy.
　　　　　S V

　　　D) She exercises every morning.
　　　　　S　　V

02 A) His dog barks loudly.
　　　　　　S　　V

　　　B) My class starts at 8:00.
　　　　　　S　　V

　　　C) There is an apple on the table.
　　　　　　　V　　S

　　　D) We always eat dinner together.
　　　　　　S　　　V

03 A) He likes vegetables.
　　　　　　S　V

　　　B) I want something to drink.
　　　　　S V

　　　C) This little black dress is expensive.
　　　　　　　　S　　　　V

　　　D) Those kids speak English.
　　　　　　S　　V

04 A) There are a lot of people on the street.
　　　　　　　V　　S

　　　B) She took the test last Friday.
　　　　　S　V

　　　C) We talked for hours.
　　　　　S　V

　　　D) The little girl likes to play at the playground.
　　　　　　　S　　　V

05 are in the library

06 smokes too much

07 The phone rang

08 Isabella lives in Boston

09 There are many people at the airport

10 I sleep at 11

정답 및 해설집

● 2형식

01 A) good   B) quickly   C) delicious   D) quick   E) beautifully
02 A) salty   B) fast   C) easily   D) wonderful   E) bitter
03 A) look   B) sounds   C) smells   D) looks   E) tastes
04 A) happy   B) terrible   C) quickly   D) angry   E) happily
05 In autumn, the leaves turn brown.
06 She became angry and yelled at the children.
07 You look really great today!
08 A) 1형식   B) 2형식   C) 2형식   D) 1형식
09 A) 2형식   B) 1형식   C) 2형식   D) 2형식
10 A) 2형식   B) 1형식   C) 2형식   D) 2형식

● 3형식

01 A) <u>Daniel</u> usually <u>drinks</u> <u>tea</u> in the morning.   B) <u>We</u> <u>parked</u> <u>the car</u> in the parking lot.
　　　 S　　　　　V　　O　　　　　　　　　　　　　　　 S　　V　　　O

　　 C) <u>My mom</u> <u>loves</u> <u>us</u> very much.   D) <u>She</u> <u>likes</u> <u>writing novels</u>.
　　　　 S　　　V　　O　　　　　　　　　　 S　　V　　　O

02 A) <u>We</u> <u>had</u> <u>a great time</u> at the party.   B) <u>I</u> usually <u>take</u> <u>a shower</u> before going to school.
　　　 S　 V　　　O　　　　　　　　　　　　　　 S　　　　V　　　O

　　 C) <u>Jack and Ron</u> <u>like</u> <u>to play basketball</u>.   D) <u>Colin</u> <u>enjoys</u> <u>running</u>.
　　　　　 S　　　　V　　　　O　　　　　　　　　 S　　V　　　O

03 A) <u>I</u> <u>opened</u> <u>the box</u> very carefully.   B) <u>Harry</u> <u>practiced</u> <u>the violin</u> every day.
　　　 S　 V　　O　　　　　　　　　　　　　　 S　　V　　　O

　　 C) <u>I</u> <u>rang</u> <u>the bell</u> a few times.   D) <u>They</u> <u>left</u> <u>a note</u> for Jack.
　　　 S　 V　　O　　　　　　　　　　　　 S　　V　　O

04 My mom cleans the house every day.
05 She enjoys reading books.
06 My friend dislikes cold weather.
07 Sally has blue eyes.
08 A) 1형식   B) 3형식   C) 2형식   D) 3형식
09 A) 3형식   B) 2형식   C) 2형식   D) 3형식
10 A) 3형식   B) 3형식   C) 1형식   D) 1형식

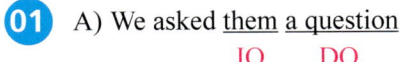

● 4형식

01 A) We asked them a question.   B) I read the baby a book.
         　　　　　IO　　DO　　　　　　　　　　　IO　　DO

　　　C) I wrote my friend a letter.   D) Can you send me a letter?
         　　　　IO　　　DO　　　　　　　　　　　　　IO　　DO

02 A) I brought Diane a balloon.   B) The students asked the teacher many questions.
         　　　　　IO　　DO　　　　　　　　　　　　　　　　IO　　　　DO

　　　C) Randy threw Robert the football.   D) Give me that book.
         　　　　　　IO　　　DO　　　　　　　　　　IO　　DO

03 A) Nicole showed us her photos.   B) Please, pass me the salt.
         　　　　　　IO　　DO　　　　　　　　　　　　　IO　　DO

　　　C) Jack gave Teo and Luna the keys.   D) Mika bought me flowers.
         　　　　　　　IO　　　　DO　　　　　　　　　　　IO　　DO

04 A) 4형식   B) 4형식   C) 4형식   D) 3형식

05 A) 4형식   B) 4형식   C) 3형식   D) 4형식

06 A) 4형식   B) 4형식   C) 3형식   D) 3형식

07 A) to   B) for   C) to   D) to

08 A) to   B) for   C) for   D) of

09 A) to   B) to   C) for   D) for

10 I often read stories to Lucy.

11 Could you pass this newspaper to Mr. Andrews?

12 Bob wrote a letter to Ann.

13 I gave Peter lunch yesterday.

14 Can I show you my photos?

15 Carol teaches children mathematics.

● 5형식

01 A) The noise drove him mad.   B) He painted the wall green.
         　　　　　　　　O　　OC　　　　　　　　　　O　　OC

　　　C) My sister named the dog Boss.   D) You make you want to cry.
         　　　　　　　　　O　　OC　　　　　　　　O　　OC

02 A) We consider the matter important.   B) Listening to this song always makes me happy.
         　　　　　　　　O　　　OC　　　　　　　　　　　　　　　　O　　OC

　　　C) Now, I call Minnesota home.   D) I found that class a challenge.
         　　　　　　　O　　　OC　　　　　　　　　　O　　　OC

정답 및 해설집

03 A) We call it friendship.
      O OC

B) My parents wouldn't allow me to go to the party.
             O   OC

C) Danny believes us honest.
       O OC

D) I saw you dancing.
     O OC

04 A) 4형식 B) 3형식 C) 5형식 D) 3형식

05 A) 3형식 B) 5형식 C) 5형식 D) 5형식

06 A) 5형식 B) 5형식 C) 3형식 D) 4형식

07 A) 3형식 B) 5형식 C) 3형식 D) 5형식

08 A) to lend B) playing C) to be D) wash

09 A) to call B) send C) watched D) help

10 A) know B) shaking C) crossing D) singing

11 I want you to be happy.

12 Nicole told me to wait for her.

13 Harry makes me laugh.

14 I saw him leave a few minutes ago.

15 Liam got her to fix his watch.

실전문제

● 1 & 2형식

01 A) comfortable 2형식 B) comfortably 1형식 C) heavily 1형식 D) heavy 2형식

02 A) polite 2형식 B) politely 1형식 C) safely 1형식 D) safe 2형식

03 A) happily 1형식 B) happy 2형식 C) well 1형식 D) well 1형식

04 A) slowly 1형식 B) true 2형식 C) terrible 2형식 D) terribly 1형식

05 ⑤ **06** ② **07** ④ **08** ③ **09** ②

10 A) well → good B) greatly → great C) calmly → calm

11 A) softly → soft B) ✗ C) deliciously → delicious

12 A) tire → tired B) loudly → loud C) diffrently → different

정답 및 해설집

13 ④: 다음 문장은 아래와 같아 바꿔야 올바른 문장이 된다.
① The cake tastes **sweet**.
② The sunset over the ocean was absolutely **lovely**.
③ The soup was too **salty**.
⑤ My new shoes are **comfortable**.

14 ②: 다음 문장은 아래와 같아 바꿔야 올바른 문장이 된다.
① The leaves turn **golden** in fall.
③ The bread is **fresh**.
④ Your sister became **happy**.
⑤ The chicken tastes **great** with barbecue sauce.

15 ①, ④, ⑥, ⑧: 다음 문장은 아래와 같아 바꿔야 올바른 문장이 된다.
② The weather feels **warm**.
③ The flowers look **lovely**.
⑤ The shampoo smells **nice**.
⑦ The boys kept **quiet**.

16 ①, ③, ⑤, ⑥: 다음 문장은 아래와 같아 바꿔야 올바른 문장이 된다.
② This blanket is **soft**.
④ The chocolate cake tastes rich and **moist**.
⑦ The music sounds **loud**.
⑧ The flowers look bright and **colorful** in the garden.

17 ④: 다음 문장은 아래와 같아 바꿔야 올바른 문장이 된다.
④ The food smells ~~like~~ spicy.

18 ①, ③: 다음 문장은 아래와 같아 바꿔야 올바른 문장이 된다.
① The music sounded very **joyful** in the concert hall.
③ The flowers smell **like** roses in the garden.

19 ⑤, ⑥, ⑦: 다음 문장은 아래와 같아 바꿔야 올바른 문장이 된다.
⑤ The steak feels tender and **juicy**.
⑥ You didn't look ~~like~~ well.
⑦ The ice cream tastes **creamy**.

20 ②, ③, ④, ⑥, ⑦: 다음 문장은 아래와 같아 바꿔야 올바른 문장이 된다.
② The water tastes **salty**.
③ She feels **bad** almost every morning.
④ He smells **good**.
⑥ The music sounds **horrible**.
⑦ The birds sing **happily**.

21 Gabriel is a student from Brazil. 2형식

22 The sun rises in the east. 1형식

23 The Olympic Games started(= began) in Greece. 1형식

24 Martin Luther King was a brave man. 2형식

25 Marie Curie was a great and smart scientist. 2형식

26 There is a puppy in the basket. 1형식

27 Nelson Mandela became the first black president. 2형식

28 Russia is the largest country on earth. 2형식
29 The leaves turned red and yellow. 2형식
30 K-pop is popular in many countries. 2형식
31 This food looks fresh and healthy. 2형식
32 Chris is working at his office. 1형식
33 Kiara is listening to music. 1형식
34 Paris is famous for the Eiffel Tower. 2형식
35 Patrick complains too much. 1형식

● 3 & 4형식

01 A) John will bring a cake to us.　　B) Mr. Jackson teaches English to us.

02 A) Sam made some pizza for us.　　B) Can you teach a new song to me?

03 A) with → ✗　　B) for → ✗　　C) ✗

04 A) for → to　　B) about → ✗　　C) about → ✗
※ B)와 C)의 동사 'mentioned'와 'discussed'는 타동사이므로 전치사 사용하지 않음

05 A) ✗　　B) you the problem → the problem to you　　C) postcard me → postcard to me

06 ④: 동사 send는 3형식으로 사용될 때 to를 사용하고, bake, find, make는 for를 사용한다.

07 ①: 동사 make는 3형식으로 사용될 때 for를 사용하고, lend, bring, read, give는 to를 사용한다.

08 ①: 동사 show는 3형식으로 사용될 때 to를 사용하고, prepare, build, buy, cook은 for를 사용한다.

09 ②: 동사 ask는 3형식으로 사용될 때 of를 사용하고, pass, sell, show, take는 to를 사용한다.

10 ④: 동사 make는 3형식으로 사용될 때 for를 사용하고, read, teach, send, promise는 to를 사용한다.

11 ⑤: 동사 do는 3형식으로 사용될 때 for를 사용하고, write, teach, sell, lend는 to를 사용한다.

12 ①: 빈칸에는 동사 get을 넣어야 한다. 동사 get은 3형식으로 사용될 때 for를 사용하고, send, give, sell, bring은 to를 사용한다.

13 ③: 빈칸에는 동사 bake를 넣어야 한다. 동사 bake는 3형식으로 사용될 때 for를 사용하고, send, give, sell, teach는 to를 사용한다.

14 ③: 빈칸에는 동사 bought을 넣어야 한다. 동사 bought는 3형식으로 사용될 때 for를 사용하고, give, send, bring, show는 to를 사용한다.

15 ③: 빈칸에 어색한 동사는 bought이다. bought는 3형식으로 사용될 때 for를 사용하고, give, send, bring, read는 to를 사용한다.

16 ①, ②, ④, ⑤: 빈칸에 어색한 동사는 gave, sent, brought, showed이며, 이 동사들은 3형식으로 사용될 때 to를 사용한다.

정답 및 해설집

17 ④: ④번은 4형식으로 어법상 올바른 문장이다. ①번은 to를 삭제, ②번은 a toy to me로, ③번은 for를 of로, ⑤번은 for를 삭제해야 올바른 문장이 된다.

18 ②, ⑤: ②번, ⑤번은 3형식으로 어법상 올바른 문장이다. ①번은 to를 삭제, ③번은 gave it to me로, ④번은 explained the problem to me.로 바꿔야 올바른 문장이 된다.

19 ③, ④: ③번은 3형식, ④번은 4형식으로 어법상 올바른 문장이다. ①번은 the package to me로, ②번은 get it for you로, ⑤번은 asked me what the problem was로 바꿔야 올바른 문장이 된다.

20 ②, ⑤: ②번의 동사 suggest는 3형식 동사이므로 suggest a good pet shop to me로, ⑤번 문장은 3형식 gave it to us로 바꿔야 올바른 문장이 된다.

21 ①, ④: ①번은 for를 to로, ④번은 for를 to로 바꿔야 올바른 문장이 된다.

22 ①, ②: ①번은 said something to me로, ②번은 find me a job으로 바꿔야 올바른 문장이 된다.

23 ④, ⑤: 〈보기〉와 ④, ⑤번은 4형식이고, ①, ②, ③번은 3형식이다.

24 ⑤: 〈보기〉와 ⑤번은 3형식이고, ①, ②, ③, ④번은 4형식이다.

25 ①, ④: ②번은 대명사를 연속해서 쓸 수 없으므로 sent it to me로, ③번의 동사 bought와 ⑤번의 동사 made는 3형식으로 사용될 때 for를 사용한다.

26 ①, ②, ③: ④번의 동사 found가 3형식으로 사용될 때 for를 사용하고, ⑤번의 동사 lend는 to를 사용한다.

27 ④: ①번은 the story to me로, ②번은 to 삭제, ③, ⑤번은 for를 삭제해야 올바른 문장이 된다.

28 ③, ④, ⑤: ①번은 for를 to로, ②번은 for를 삭제해야 올바른 문장이 된다.

29 ⑤: ①번은 for를 to로, ②번은 to를 for로, ③번은 of를 to로, ④번은 to를 for로 바꿔야 올바른 문장이 된다.

30 ①, ④, ⑤: ②번은 to를 for로, ③번은 for를 to로 바꿔야 올바른 문장이 된다.

31 ①, ②, ③, ⑤: ④번은 for를 to로 바꿔야 올바른 문장이 된다.

32 ①, ⑤: ②번은 to를 for로, ③, ④번은 for를 to로 바꿔야 올바른 문장이 된다.

33 A) She bought a house for her daughter.   B) He lent some money to her.
C) We gave some money to them.

34 A) They built a tree-house for their children.   B) Can you bring the newspaper to me?
C) Can you get my hat for me?

35 A) They promised many things to me.   B) Mom read a story to me.
C) Let's take some flowers to her.

36 A) I'll tell the truth to you.   B) He showed the photo to me.
C) We bought a present for Jane.

정답 및 해설집

37 A) Can you teach me a new song? B) He wrote me a poem.
C) Can you bring her some water?

38 A) She asked me a question. B) He taught them English.
C) We bought the boy a computer.

39 A) We cooked the children spaghetti. B) Dave showed him his photos.
C) Jack told me the story.

40 A) Kate found me the lost wallet. B) He did James a favor.
C) Her dad told her something important.

41 Bill doesn't like vegetables. **42** I broke my arm last month.

43 She has her earrings on her ears. **44** He drinks coffee in the morning.

45 We shouldn't feed wild animals. **46** Did you pass the test?

47 Jim is learning Japanese. **48** Beethoven wrote many famous pieces of music.

49 Alexander Graham Bell invented the telephone. **50** We could see the ocean from the hotel.

51 3형식: Sam is making dinner for us. 4형식: Sam is making us dinner.

52 3형식: Please show your passport to me. 4형식: Please show me your passport.

53 3형식: I have to buy a new wallet for my mom. 4형식: I have to buy my mom a new wallet.

54 3형식: Joe often asks many questions of me. 4형식: Joe often asks me many questions.

55 3형식: I lent $30 to Nicole yesterday. 4형식: I lent Nicole $30 yesterday.

56 3형식: Will you get some bread for me? 4형식: Will you get me some bread?

57 3형식: Miss Yuki teaches Japanese to students. 4형식: Miss Yuki teaches students Japanese.

58 3형식: My mom reads stories to me every night. 4형식: My mom reads me stories every night.

59 3형식: Fatima often gives flowers to her mother. 4형식: Fatima often gives her mother flowers.

60 3형식: They will build a house for their parents. 4형식: They will build their parents a house.

● 5형식

01 ①: 문장 구조 [주어+advise+목적어+not+to 동사 원형]

02 ①, ④: 문장 구조 [주어+help+목적어+(to) 동사 원형]

03 ④: 문장 구조 [주어+tell+목적어+to 동사 원형]

정답 및 해설집

04 ④ : 문장 구조 [주어+let+목적어+동사 원형]

05 ⑤ : 문장 구조 [주어+expect+목적어+to 동사 원형]

06 ① : 문장 구조 [주어+order+목적어+to 동사 원형]

07 ② : 문장 구조 [주어+don't allow+목적어+to 동사 원형]

08 ③ : 문장 구조 [주어+expect+목적어+to 동사 원형]

09 ② : 문장 구조 [주어+get+목적어+to 동사 원형]

10 ④ : 문장 구조 [주어+ask+목적어+to 동사 원형]

11 ② : 문장 구조 [주어+encourage+목적어+to 동사 원형]

12 ① : 문장 구조 [주어+allow+목적어+to 동사 원형], who are family members는 people를 수식한다.

13 ⑤ : 문장 구조 [주어+ask+목적어+to 동사 원형]

14 ③ : 문장 구조 [주어+allow+목적어+to 동사 원형] 종속절에 was라는 과거 시제가 있으므로 현재 시제 persuades는 사용할 수 없다.

15 ① : 문장 구조 [주어+motivate+목적어+to 동사 원형]

16 ① : 문장 구조 [주어+want+목적어+to 동사 원형]

17 ② : 문장 구조 [주어+get+목적어+to 동사 원형]

18 ①, ② : 문장 구조 [주어+help+목적어+(to) 동사 원형]

19 ② : 문장 구조 [주어+tell+목적어+to 동사 원형]

20 ② : 문장 구조 [주어+expect+목적어+to 동사 원형]를 사용하므로 빈칸에 적절하지 못하다.

21 ⑤ : 문장 구조 [주어+allow+목적어+to 동사 원형]를 사용하므로 빈칸에 적절하지 못하다.

22 ①, ②, ⑤ : 문장 구조 [주어+(준)사역동사+목적어+동사 원형]을 사용하므로 빈칸에 적절하지 못하다.

23 ①, ② : [주어+help+목적어+(to) 동사 원형]의 문장 구조를 사용한다. 주어가 3인칭 단수이므로 동사에 –s를 사용해야 한다.

24 ② : asked '간청했다'는 과거 시제이며, 문장 구조 [주어+ask+목적어+to 동사 원형]을 사용한다. 부정어는 to 원형 부정사 앞에 사용한다.

25 ④ : persuaded '설득했다'는 과거 시제이며, 문장 구조 [주어+persuade+목적어+to 동사 원형]을 사용한다.

26 ③, ④, ⑤ : ①번 문장은 [주어+cause+목적어+to 동사 원형]의 구조로 lose 앞에 to를 넣어야 되고, ②번 문장은 [주어+allow+목적어+to 동사 원형]의 구조로 going을 to go로 바꿔야 올바른 문장이 된다.

27 ①, ②, ③, ⑤ : ④번 문장은 [주어+hear+목적어+목적격 보어]의 구조로 목적격 보어로는 동사 원형 또는 현재 분사(-ing)를 써야 올바른 문장이 된다. 따라서 to go를 go 또는 going으로 고쳐야 올바른 문장이 된다.

정답 및 해설집

28 ③, ⑤ : ③번의 문장 구조 [주어+let+목적어+동사 원형]
⑤번의 문장 구조 [주어+advise+목적어+not+to 동사 원형]

29 ③ : ③번의 문장 구조 [주어+invite+목적어+to 동사 원형]

30 ⑤ : (A)의 문장 구조 [주어+want+목적어+to 동사 원형]
(B)의 문장 구조 [주어+advise+목적어+to 동사 원형]
(C)의 문장 구조 [주어+force+목적어+to 동사 원형]
(D)의 문장 구조 [주어+get+목적어(사람)+to 동사 원형]

31 The joke made him angry.
32 Louise will paint the wall blue.
33 Helen asked us to be quiet.
34 We saw the girls dancing.
35 She has her clothes washed every week.
36 Let me sleep under the tree.
37 I advised her to study for the exam.
38 We elected him president.
39 She heard a baby cry(crying) in the next room.
40 He got his daughter to clean the room.
41 Do you want me to go with you to the beach?
42 Kate told her friend to meet her at the café.
43 I had my brother carry my suitcase.
44 Can you help me plant flowers next Saturday?
45 My parents listen to birds singing every morning.

● 종합문제

01 A) 1 B) 2 C) 3 D) 4 E) 1
02 A) 5 B) 5 C) 1 D) 3 E) 1
03 A) 1 B) 4 C) 2 D) 3 E) 1
04 A) 1 B) 5 C) 2 D) 3 E) 5
05 A) 4 B) 5 C) 2 D) 3 E) 5
06 There is a clock on the wall.
07 The train arrived early.
08 It snows a lot in winter in Hokkaido, Japan.
09 Somebody is swimming in the lake.
10 Everyone is special in many ways.
11 The wind feels cool on my face.
12 Kate looks well and happy.
13 It gets dark very early here in winter.
14 Dad is washing the dishes.
15 Ann plays tennis once a week.
16 Can you bring her some water?
17 We would like to build Katie a playhouse.
18 This book made her famous.
19 I want you to learn English.
20 Let me have a look at that letter.

꼭 알아야 하는 영문법
8품사 workbook

정답 및 해설집

01 명사: John, Austria, pig, sadness, death, South America

02 대명사: him, we, you, them

03 동사: speak, write, sing

04 형용사: young, cold, useful, great

05 부사: badly, here, always, slowly

06 전치사: of, at, about

07 접속사: but, because, or

08 감탄사: oops, hey

09 A) She is　　B) He is　　C) She is　　D) They are

10 A) We are　　B) It is　　C) They are　　D) I am

11 A) They are　　B) They are　　C) It is　　D) You are

12 A) You are　　B) It is　　C) They are　　D) I am

13 A) We are　　B) She is　　C) He is　　D) They are

14 A) He, her　　B) It　　C) them, They　　D) me, them

15 A) mine　　B) ours　　C) them　　D) He, it

16 A) his　　B) They　　C) She, us (= me), We　　D) yours

17 A) he, it　　B) They, theirs　　C) hers　　D) They

18 A) yours　　B) they　　C) her, mine　　D) it

19 ③: ③번의 colored는 동사로서 '색을 칠했다'의 의미이지만, 나머지는 명사로 '색'의 의미이다.

20 ⑤: ⑤번의 well은 형용사로서 '건강한'의 의미이지만, 나머지는 부사로 '잘'의 의미이다.

21 ①: ①번의 work는 동사로서 '일하다'의 의미이지만, 나머지는 명사로 '일'의 의미이다.

22 ④: ④번의 broke는 동사로서 '깼다'의 의미이지만, 나머지는 명사로 '휴식' 또는 '쉬는 시간'의 의미이다.

23 ③: ③번의 change는 명사로서 '변화'의 의미이지만, 나머지는 동사로 '변화하다' 또는 '바꾸다'의 의미이다.

24 ③: ③번의 fair는 명사로서 '박람회'의 의미이지만, 나머지는 형용사로 '공정한'의 의미이다.

25 ⑤: ⑤번의 pretty는 부사로서 '꽤'의 의미이지만, 나머지는 형용사로 '예쁜'의 의미이다.

26 ③: ③번의 ordered는 동사로서 '주문했다'의 의미이지만, 나머지는 명사로 '주문'의 의미이다.

정답 및 해설집

27 ④: ④번의 face는 명사로서 '얼굴'의 의미이지만, 나머지는 동사로 '직면하다' 또는 '마주하다'의 의미이다.

28 ②: ②번의 fly는 명사로서 '파리'의 의미이지만, 나머지는 동사로 '날다'의 의미이다.

29 ④: ④번의 fast는 형용사로서 '빠른'의 의미이지만, 나머지는 부사로 '빠르게'의 의미이다.

30 ②: ②번의 right는 명사로서 '권리'의 의미이지만, 나머지는 형용사로 '오른쪽의' 의미이다.

31 ③: ③번의 train은 명사로서 '기차'의 의미이지만, 나머지는 동사로 '훈련시키다' 또는 '훈련하다'의 의미이다.

32 ②: ②번의 race는 동사로서 '경주하다'의 의미이지만, 나머지는 명사로 '경주' 또는 '(달리기) 시합'의 의미이다.

33 ①: ①번의 present는 형용사로서 '현재의' 의미이지만, 나머지는 명사로 '선물'의 의미이다.

34 ③: ③번의 run은 명사로서 '달리기'의 의미이지만, 나머지는 동사로 '뛰다'의 의미이다.

35 ②: ②번의 last는 동사로서 '견디다' 또는 '지속하다'의 의미이지만, 나머지는 형용사로 '마지막' 또는 '최종의' 의미이다.

36 ③: ③번의 book은 명사로서 '책'의 의미이지만, 나머지는 동사로 '예약하다'의 의미이다.

37 ④: ④번의 mean은 형용사로서 '못된' 또는 '심술궂은'의 의미이지만, 나머지는 동사로 '의미하다'의 의미이다.

38 ④: ④번의 plant는 명사로서 '식물'의 의미이지만, 나머지는 동사로 '(식물을) 심다'의 의미이다.

39 명사: 1. Justin Bieber   2. singer   3. fans   4. songs   5. people   6. fans   7. music   8. performances   9. Justin   10. clothes   11. sunglasses   12. concerts   13. audience

40 대명사: 1. This   2. him   3. him

[39-40] **Justin Bieber** is a famous **singer** with a lot of **fans**. His **songs** are loved by many **people**. The **fans** enjoy his **music** and his **performances**. **Justin** often wears cool **clothes** and **sunglasses**. **This** makes **him** look stylish. At **concerts**, the **audience** sings along with **him** and cheers loudly.

41 1. is   2. has   3. watch   4. are   5. are   6. love

The Premier League **is** a well-known soccer league in England. It **has** many great teams like Manchester United, Liverpool, and Tottenham Hotspur. People all over the world **watch** the games. The matches **are** very exciting and the players **are** very skilled. Fans **love** to see their favorite teams win.

42 1. Great   2. famous   3. many   4. long   5. many   6. long   7. different   8. Great   9. popular   10. rich

The **Great** Wall of China is a **famous** landmark that attracts **many** visitors. It was built a **long** time ago to protect China from invaders. Construction started more than 2,000 years ago and continued for **many** centuries. The Wall is very **long**, stretching over 13,000 miles. It is made of **different** materials like earth, wood, and stone. Today, the **Great** Wall is a **popular** place for tourists and a symbol of China's **rich** history.

정답 및 해설집

43 1. Today   2. very   3. carefully   4. perfectly   5. happily   6. incredibly
7. even   8. really   9. definitely

Today, I enjoyed a **very** tasty and special meal. Mom **carefully** cooked the rice, which was hot and soft, and it went **perfectly** with spicy kimchi and delicious side dishes. I **happily** ate crispy fish with fresh, crunchy lettuce. The fish was **incredibly** moist and flavorful, and the homemade sauce made it **even** more delightful. For dessert, I had sweet and juicy fruits that tasted **really** refreshing. It was a wonderful end to a **definitely** great meal.

44 1. for   2. in   3. of   4. for   5. to   6. on   7. about   8. for   9. with   10. around   11. about

Elon Musk is renowned **for** his work **in** technology and space. He is the founder **of** SpaceX, where he builds rockets **for** traveling **to** space. Additionally, he started Tesla, which makes electric cars to promote a cleaner environment. While he works **on** these projects, he also thinks **about** new ideas **for** the future. Because he wants to help solve major problems, he often shares his plans **with** the public. Consequently, many people **around** the world are excited **about** his work and achievements.

45 1. and   2. when   3. and   4. so   5. and   6. Although   7. and   8. and   9. but

Last summer, we went on a wonderful trip to Italy, **and** it was an unforgettable experience. We visited the ancient Colosseum in Rome. We also had a chance to explore charming little towns in Tuscany **when** we traveled by car. We stayed in a lovely place with a beautiful view of the countryside. Each day, we tried new foods **and** experienced different cultures, **so** every moment felt exciting **and** new. **Although** the trip was filled with amazing sights **and** activities, we still wished we could have stayed longer. We ended our trip in Venice. For our final activity, we took a romantic gondola ride through the canals, **and** it was a perfect way to conclude our journey. The entire trip was amazing, **but** it went by quickly. I'm already looking forward to my next adventure.

46 1. Wow   2. Oh   3. Ah

Wow, the weather is great today! The sky is clear, and the sunshine is warm. **Oh**, listen to the birds chirping. **Ah**, it's a waste to stay home on a day like this. The blooming flowers and playful puppies are so cute. It's a truly happy day!

47 A) Paris: 명사   B) stands: 동사   C) many: 형용사
D) tourists: 명사   E) lively: 형용사   F) with: 전치사

48 G) shines: 동사   H) brightly: 부사   I) walking: 명사(동명사)
J) along: 전치사   K) and: 접속사   L) architecture: 명사

49 A) diverse   품사: 형용사   의미: 다양한   B) It   품사: 대명사   의미: 그것(지구)
C) around   품사: 전치사   의미: 주위에, 주변에

정답 및 해설집

50
- D) varies 품사: 동사 의미: 다르다, 다양하다
- E) greatly 품사: 부사 의미: 크게, 매우
- F) from 품사: 전치사 의미: ~로부터

51
- G) place 품사: 명사 의미: 장소
- H) while 품사: 접속사 의미: 반면에
- I) cold 품사: 형용사 의미: 추운

52
- J) variety 품사: 명사 의미: 다양성
- K) plants 품사: 명사 의미: 식물
- L) provides 품사: 동사 의미: 제공하다

53
- A) K-pop 품사: 명사 의미: 케이팝, 한국 대중음악
- B) popular 품사: 형용사 의미: 인기 있는, 대중적인
- C) genre 품사: 명사 의미: 장르

54
- D) mixes 품사: 동사 의미: 섞다
- E) features 품사: 동사 의미: 특징을 이루다, 포함하다
- F) energetic 품사: 형용사 의미: 활기찬

55
- G) moves 품사: 명사 의미: 동작, 움직임
- H) work 품사: 동사 의미: 일하다, 노력하다
- I) unique 품사: 형용사 의미: 독특한, 유일한

56
- J) influence 품사: 명사 의미: 영향력
- K) is growing 품사: 동사 의미: 증가하고 있다, 성장하고 있다
- L) global 품사: 형용사 의미: 세계적인

57 A) difficulty → difficult   B) success → successful   C) importance → important

58 A) living → life   B) sign → signature   C) We → They

59 A) me → I   B) "Don't late." → "Don't be late."   C) clear → clearly

60 A) she → her   B) It was → They were   C) It's → its

61 ①, ③: 〈보기〉와 ①, ③번은 형용사로서 '인색한'의 의미이지만, 나머지는 동사로 '~를 의미하다'이다.

62 ③, ④, ⑥, ⑦: 본문의 like와 같은 의미로 쓰인 것은 ③, ④, ⑥, ⑦번이다.
① 런던에서의 생활은 마음에 드나요? (런던 생활을 얼마나 좋아하나요?) (동사)
② 나는 그가 아이들한테 소리 지르는 방식을 좋아하지 않는다. (동사)
③ 이 스웨터는 내가 집에 가지고 있는 스웨터처럼 부드러워요. (전치사)
④ 그녀의 목소리가 가수처럼 들려요. (전치사)
⑤ 그는 등 뒤에서 사람들에 대해 얘기하는 걸 절대로 좋아하지 않는다. (동사)
⑥ 고양이는 다른 애완동물처럼 친근하다. (전치사)
⑦ 이 책은 지난번에 읽은 거처럼 재미있다. (전치사)
⑧ 내가 존을 좋아하는 이유 중 하나는 그의 유머 감각이다. (동사)

정답 및 해설집

63 ①, ③, ④, ⑦: 본문의 (A) <u>work</u>와 같은 의미로 쓰인 것은 ①, ③, ④, ⑦번이다.
① 갤러리에는 여러 현대 예술가들의 작품이 전시되어 있습니다. (명사)
② 젊은이들이 일을 찾아 도시로 옵니다. (명사)
③ 그의 최근 작품은 걸작이다. (명사)
④ 그들은 장인의 세밀한 작품에 감탄했다. (명사)
⑤ 우리는 이 프로젝트를 완성하기 위해 함께 일한다. (동사)
⑥ 이 시기에는 일이 많지 않다. (명사)
⑦ 이 소설은 그의 가장 위대한 작품 중 하나로 간주된다. (명사)
⑧ 우리는 같은 회사에서 일한다. (동사)

64 ②, ③, ④, ⑤: 본문의 (B) <u>bold</u>와 같은 의미로 쓰인 것은 ②, ③, ④, ⑤번이다.
① 모든 제목은 그들이 읽기 쉽게 볼 수 있도록 굵은 글씨로 되어 있다. (형용사)
② 회의에서 목소리를 내기로 한 그의 대담한 선택은 모두에게 깊은 인상을 주었습니다. (형용사)
③ 그녀는 자신의 진로를 완전히 바꾸는 대담한 선택을 했다. (형용사)
④ 혼자 전국을 여행하겠다는 그의 대담한 아이디어는 흥미진진했다. (형용사)
⑤ 새로운 재료를 시도한 셰프의 대담한 결정이 독특한 요리를 만들었다. (형용사)
⑥ 제목은 눈에 띄게 하기 위해 굵은 글씨로 되어 있었다. (형용사)
⑦ 중요한 요점을 강조하기 위해 굵은 글씨로 써져 있다. (형용사)

꼭 알아야 하는 영문법
문장성분과 5형식 workbook

정답 및 해설집

01 A) <u>William</u> <u>eats</u> too much.　　　B) <u>The phone</u> <u>rang</u> repeatedly.
　　　　　S　　　V　　　　　　　　　　　　　　S　　　　V

　　　C) <u>A lot of people</u> <u>went</u> there.
　　　　　　　S　　　　　　V

02 A) <u>Charlie</u> <u>goes</u> to school every day.　　B) <u>Your essay</u> <u>reads</u> well.
　　　　　S　　　V　　　　　　　　　　　　　　　　S　　　　V

　　　C) <u>The train</u> <u>arrived</u> early this morning.
　　　　　　S　　　　V

03 A) <u>The cat</u> <u>sleeps</u> on the couch.　　B) <u>They</u> <u>swim</u> in the lake.
　　　　　S　　　V　　　　　　　　　　　　　　S　　V

　　　C) <u>The dog</u> <u>barks</u> at strangers.
　　　　　　S　　　V

04 A) <u>Frank</u> <u>is</u> <u>an architect</u>.　　B) <u>Alice</u> <u>looked</u> <u>cute</u> yesterday.
　　　　　S　　V　　C　　　　　　　　　　　S　　　V　　C

　　　C) <u>The soup</u> <u>tastes</u> <u>horrible</u>.
　　　　　　S　　　V　　　C

05 A) <u>The sky</u> <u>appeared</u> <u>clear</u> today.　　B) <u>The room</u> <u>seemed</u> <u>cozy</u> last night.
　　　　　S　　　V　　　C　　　　　　　　　　　S　　　V　　　C

　　　C) <u>The cookies</u> baking in the oven <u>smell</u> <u>delicious</u>.
　　　　　　S　　　　　　　　　　　　　　V　　　C

06 A) <u>The water</u> <u>felt</u> <u>cold</u> this morning.　　B) <u>The music</u> <u>sounded</u> <u>amazing</u> at the concert.
　　　　　S　　　V　　C　　　　　　　　　　　　　S　　　V　　　C

　　　C) <u>The child</u> <u>looked</u> <u>excited</u> on his birthday.
　　　　　　S　　　V　　　C

07 A) <u>Betty</u> <u>parked</u> <u>the car</u> in the car park.　　B) <u>We</u> <u>took</u> <u>her</u> to the station.
　　　　　S　　V　　　O　　　　　　　　　　　　　　S　　V　　O

　　　C) <u>We</u> <u>enjoyed</u> <u>ourselves</u> at the party.
　　　　　S　　V　　　O

08 A) <u>I</u> <u>want</u> <u>to sleep</u> now.　　B) <u>Kate</u> <u>enjoys</u> <u>playing tennis</u>.
　　　　S　V　　O　　　　　　　　　　　S　　V　　　O

　　　C) <u>Martin</u> <u>introduced</u> <u>his guests</u> to us.
　　　　　S　　　V　　　　　O

정답 및 해설집

09 A) <u>Gerald</u> <u>explained</u> <u>the situation</u> to me.　　B) <u>Don't say</u> <u>it</u> to him.
　　　　S　　　V　　　　O　　　　　　　　　　　　　V　　O　(부정 명령문이므로 주어 You 생략됨)

　　C) Would <u>you</u> <u>describe</u> <u>it</u> for me, please?
　　　　　　　S　　　V　　O

10 A) We gave <u>Sam</u> <u>a good watch</u>.　　B) I sent <u>Mike</u> <u>a parcel</u> last week.
　　　　　　　　IO　　　DO　　　　　　　　　　　　IO　　　DO

　　C) They offered <u>her</u> <u>a promotion</u> at work.
　　　　　　　　　　IO　　　DO

11 A) I brought <u>my friend</u> <u>a souvenir</u> from the trip.
　　　　　　　　IO　　　　DO

　　B) He showed <u>us</u> <u>his new painting</u>.
　　　　　　　　IO　　　DO

　　C) The teacher gives <u>the students</u> <u>extra homework</u> almost every day.
　　　　　　　　　　　　IO　　　　　DO

12 A) She baked <u>her neighbor</u> <u>a cake</u> for her birthday.
　　　　　　　　IO　　　　DO

　　B) He lent <u>his brother</u> <u>some money</u>.
　　　　　　　IO　　　　DO

　　C) We served <u>our guests</u> <u>a delicious meal</u> for the celebration.
　　　　　　　　IO　　　　DO

13 A) <u>Loud music</u> <u>drives</u> <u>me</u> <u>crazy</u>.　　B) <u>They</u> <u>called</u> <u>him</u> <u>foolish</u>.
　　　　S　　　V　　O　OC　　　　　　　　S　　V　　O　OC

　　C) <u>We</u> <u>appointed</u> <u>her</u> <u>chairperson</u>.
　　　　S　　　V　　　O　　　OC

14 A) <u>Keep</u> <u>it</u> <u>short</u>, please.
　　　　V　O　OC　(명령문이므로 주어 You 생략됨)

　　B) <u>His jokes</u> <u>made</u> <u>us</u> <u>laugh</u> all night.
　　　　S　　　V　　O　OC

　　C) <u>The news</u> <u>made</u> <u>her</u> <u>happy</u> this morning.
　　　　S　　　V　　O　OC

15 A) <u>They</u> <u>elected</u> <u>him</u> <u>president</u>.　　B) <u>The movie</u> <u>left</u> <u>us</u> <u>speechless</u> with its twist ending.
　　　　S　　V　　O　　OC　　　　　　　　　　S　　V　O　OC

　　C) <u>Sarah</u> <u>let</u> <u>her son</u> <u>decide</u> for himself.
　　　　S　　V　　O　　OC

16 A) 1형식　　B) 1형식　　C) 2형식　　D) 3형식

17 A) 1형식　　B) 2형식　　C) 3형식　　D) 1형식

18 A) 1형식　　B) 3형식　　C) 1형식　　D) 2형식

정답 및 해설집

19 A) 3형식　　B) 2형식　　C) 1형식　　D) 3형식
20 A) 2형식　　B) 2형식　　C) 3형식　　D) 1형식
21 A) 4형식　　B) 5형식　　C) 3형식　　D) 3형식
22 A) 3형식　　B) 4형식　　C) 5형식　　D) 3형식
23 A) 3형식　　B) 4형식　　C) 4형식　　D) 3형식
24 A) 5형식　　B) 5형식　　C) 5형식　　D) 3형식
25 A) 5형식　　B) 3형식　　C) 5형식　　D) 5형식

종합문제

26 A) 1형식　B) 2형식　C) 5형식　D) 3형식　E) 5형식
27 A) 5형식　B) 1형식　C) 4형식　D) 1형식　E) 5형식
28 A) 1형식　B) 3형식　C) 5형식　D) 1형식　E) 3형식
29 A) 1형식　B) 5형식　C) 2형식　D) 3형식　E) 4형식
30 A) 3형식　B) 5형식　C) 2형식　D) 4형식　E) 5형식
31 A) 1형식　B) 3형식　C) 3형식　D) 4형식　E) 2형식
32 A) 3형식　B) 3형식　C) 1형식　D) 2형식　E) 5형식
33 A) 3형식　B) 2형식　C) 1형식　D) 1형식　E) 4형식
34 A) 3형식　B) 5형식　C) 1형식　D) 5형식　E) 1형식
35 A) 3형식　B) 2형식　C) 1형식　D) 3형식　E) 5형식

36 1형식　　주어: She　　동사: sings
　수식어 (부사): beautifully

37 4형식　　주어: She　　동사: gave
　간접목적어: me　　직접목적어: a book　　수식어(형용사절): that she likes

38 1형식　　주어: The sun　　동사: rises
　수식어 (부사구): in the east every morning

39 2형식　　주어: This exercise　　동사: is
　수식어 (부사): extremely　　주격보어: exhausting

정답 및 해설집

40 5형식 주어: I 동사: have seen
목적어: her 목적격 보어: dancing

41 2형식 주어: I 동사: am
주격보어: interested 수식어(전치사구): in sports

42 3형식 주어: I 동사: called
목적어: John 수식어 (부사절): Before I went out

43 5형식 주어: Hot weather 동사: makes
목적어: me 목적격 보어: feel tired

44 3형식 주어: Her mother 동사: suggested
목적어(목적어 역할을 하는 명사절): that she should go and see the doctor

45 3형식 주어: We 동사: decided
목적어: not to play baseball 수식어 (전치사구): because of the weather

46 4형식 주어: (You) – 생략된 주어 동사: Show
간접목적어: me 직접목적어: how to do it

47 1형식 주어: We 동사: are leaving
수식어(부사): tomorrow

48 3형식 주어: I 동사: wonder
목적어(목적어 역할을 하는 명사절): if you could help me

49 1형식 주어: We 동사구: went out
수식어(전치사구): in spite of the rain

50 2형식 주어: all the post offices 동사: were
주격보어: closed 수식어(부사절): Since it was a national holiday